**For A Free Copy Of Our
Complete Book Catalog, Write:**

EDEN PRESS

P.O. Box 8410 Fountain Valley,
CA 92728

RECESSION- AND DEPRESSION-

PROOF

CAREERS AND BUSINESSES

BOOKS BY THE AUTHOR

Recession- and Depressionproof Careers and Businesses

Secrets of Selling by Using Spiritual Powers

Source credit: the career text was furnished by the *Occupational Outlook Handbook* and *Dictionary of Occupational Titles* (U.S. Government Printing Office).

Published by:

Kessinger Publishing Company
P.O. Box 8933
Boise, ID 83707

(See back page for ordering information.)

ISBN 0-922802-02-5

CAVEAT

While the conclusions presented in this book are based upon reasonable assumptions, no one can foresee with exact certainty all the economic, political, social, and technological forces that will ultimately affect businesses and employment. This publication provides the author's opinion regarding the subject matter covered. It is sold with the understanding that the publisher and author is not engaged in rendering legal, accounting, or other professional service. If legal advice or other expert assistance is required, the services of a competent professional should be sought.

The author and publisher specifically disclaims any personal liability, loss, or risk incurred as a consequence of the use and application, either directly or indirectly, of any advice or information presented herein.

A listing in this book is not an endorsement of a particular organization. Each is included for its subject orientation, resource potential, and willingness to share information and expertise.

RECESSION- AND DEPRESSION-

PROOF

CAREERS AND BUSINESSES

CONTENTS

INTRODUCTION

THE ODDS ARE AGAINST YOU.

Ominous government deficits, stock market meltdowns, widespread bank failures, depressed farm prices, wholesale bankruptcies, ravenous inflation, intense foreign competition, labor strikes, spending reductions, volatile interest rates, hostile corporate take-overs, crippling governmental regulations, oppressive tax increases, rising costs, and technological changes are just a few of the hundreds of adverse economic arrows that shoot down your chances of being employed.

FORTUNATELY, YOU CAN BEAT THE ODDS!

Discover *Recession- and Depressionproof Careers and Businesses* that reward you with:

* ***Steady Employment***

* ***Constant Pay***

* ***Security***

— regardless of the economy. Imagine the unlimited advantages of receiving a recession- and depressionproof income!

WHY THESE CAREERS AND BUSINESSES ARE RECESSION- AND DEPRESSIONPROOF:

— They provide essential human services.

— They are not tied to economic or business cycles.

— They are not affected by foreign competition.

— They are not eliminated due to spending reductions.

— They have survived all recessions and depressions in the past.

THE BENEFITS OF WORKING IN A RECESSION- AND DEPRESSION- PROOF OCCUPATION:

1. Your chances of being steadily employed and financially secure will dramatically increase.

2. Even if you lose your job, your odds of finding employment elsewhere, in the same occupation, will be excellent.

3. You will also discover entire industries that are recession- and depressionproof. Your financial security increases even more when you combine these **industries** with recession- and depressionproof **occupations!**

EXAMPLES

Recession- and Depressionproof		
Occupation +	**Industry** =	**Financial Security**
Lawyer	Utilities	Utilities Lawyer
Secretary	Medical	Medical Secretary
Accountant	Insurance	Insurance Accountant

GET PAID IN GOOD TIMES AND BAD.

Read this book and discover how you can protect your income by working in:

RECESSION- AND DEPRESSIONPROOF CAREERS AND BUSINESSES

WHERE TO GO FOR MORE INFORMATION

LIBRARIES have a great deal of material. Begin your library search by looking in the card catalog under "vocations," "careers," or "businesses" and then under specific fields. Check the periodical section, where you will find trade and professional magazines and journals written for people in specific occupations.

COUNSELORS can provide vocational testing and counseling. They work in:

— Guidance offices in high schools.

— Career planning and placement offices in colleges.

— Placement offices in private vocational/technical schools and institutes.

— Vocational rehabilitation agencies.

— Community organizations.

— Private counseling agencies or private practices.

— State employment service offices affiliated with the U.S. Employment Service.

PERSONAL CONTACTS are useful. Talk with people in the occupation you are considering. Find out what type of training is required, how they entered the occupation and advanced in it, and what they like and dislike about the work.

THE STATE EMPLOYMENT SERVICE, sometimes called Job Service, operates in coordination with the Department of Labor U.S. Employment Service. Its 2,000 local offices, also known as employment service centers, help job seekers locate employment and help employers find qualified workers without charge. To find the office nearest you, look in the state government telephone listings under "Job Service" or "Employment."

PRIVATE EMPLOYMENT AGENCIES can be very helpful. Most agencies operate on a commission basis, with the fee dependent upon a successful match. The fee may be paid by either the applicant or the hiring firm. If you will be responsible for the fee, find out the exact cost before using the service.

AMERICAN ENTREPRENEURS ASSOCIATION
2311 Pontius Avenue
Los Angeles, CA 90064

Sells start-up information for numerous small businesses. Write for a current catalog and price list.

AMERICAN FRANCHISE ASSOCIATION
2730 Wilshire Boulevard, Suite 400
Santa Monica, CA 90403

Provides information for franchise owners.

NATIONAL ASSOCIATION OF HOME-BASED BUSINESSES
P.O. Box 30220
Baltimore, MD 21270

Furnishes information on how to start home-based businesses.

NATIONAL ASSOCIATION OF TRADE AND TECHNICAL SCHOOLS
P.O. Box 10429
Rockville, MD 20850

Write for a free copy of the *Handbook of Accredited Private Trade and Technical Schools*. This is a useful resource for anyone considering a vocational trade.

NATIONAL HOME STUDY COUNCIL
1601 18th Street, NW
Washington, DC 20009

Write for a free copy of the *Directory of Accredited Home Study Schools*. This directory provides information about home study (correspondence) programs.

U.S. SMALL BUSINESS ADMINISTRATION
Office of Business Development
1441 L Street, NW
Washington, DC 20416

Provides useful information on starting a small business.

ABOUT GOVERNMENT JOBS

With the exception of the armed forces, law enforcement, and firefighting, government occupations were purposely excluded from this book. If you are interested in working for the government, contact the appropriate governmental agency's personnel department.

Beware! Not all government jobs are safe. During the next depression, thousands of government employees may be shocked to find themselves standing in crowded unemployment lines, while others may have to accept substantial pay cuts. Anything can happen during the next depression!

Recession- and Depressionproof

CAREERS

(Most of these occupations can also be **businesses**. For example, accountants may work for accounting firms or they may be self-employed.)

ACCOUNTANTS AND AUDITORS

Accountants and auditors prepare, analyze, and verify financial reports that furnish information to individuals, businesses, and government organizations. The major fields are: public, management, government accounting, and internal auditing. Public accountants have their own businesses or work for accounting firms. Management accountants, also called industrial or private accountants, handle the financial records of their companies. Government accountants and auditors maintain and examine the records of government agencies and audit private businesses and individuals whose dealings are subject to government regulations. Internal auditors verify the accuracy of their firm's financial records and check for waste or fraud. Within each field, accountants often concentrate on one phase of accounting. For example, many public accountants are employed primarily in financial auditing (examining a client's financial records and reports and attesting that they are in conformity with standards of preparation and reporting). Others concentrate on tax matters, such as preparing income tax returns and advising clients of the tax advantages and disadvantages of certain business decisions. Still others concentrate on consulting and offer advice on a variety of matters. They might develop or revise an accounting system to serve the needs of clients more effectively or give advice about how to manage cash resources more profitably. Management accountants, the largest group of accountants and auditors, provide the financial information executives need to make sound business decisions. They also may prepare financial reports to meet the public disclosure requirements of various stock exchanges, the Securities and Exchange Commission, and other regulatory bodies. They may work in areas such as taxation, budgeting, costs, or investments. Internal auditing is rapidly growing in importance as top management must increasingly base its decisions on reports and records rather than personal observation. Internal auditors examine and evaluate their firms' financial and informational systems, management procedures, and internal controls to ensure that records are accurate and controls are adequate to protect against fraud and waste. They also review company operations evaluating their efficiency, effectiveness, and compliance with corporate policies and procedures, laws, and government regulations. Accountants and auditors also work for federal, state and local governments, or in financial management, financial institution examination, and budget administration. In addition, a small number of persons trained as accountants staff the faculties of business and professional schools as accounting teachers, researchers, or administrators. Some work part time as accountants or consultants.

AMERICAN ACCOUNTING ASSOCIATION
5717 Bessie Drive
Sarasota, FL 33583

AMERICAN INSTITUTE OF CERTIFIED PUBLIC ACCOUNTANTS
1211 Avenue of the Americas
New York, NY 10036

ASSOCIATED REGIONAL ACCOUNTING FIRMS
1800 Century Boulevard, NE, Suite 950
Atlanta, GA 30345

INSTITUTE OF INTERNAL AUDITORS
249 Maitland Avenue
Altamonte Springs, FL 32701

NATIONAL ASSOCIATION OF ACCOUNTANTS
Ten Paragon Drive
Montvale, NJ 07645

NATIONAL SOCIETY OF PUBLIC ACCOUNTANTS
1010 North Fairfax Street
Alexandria, VA 22314

ARMED FORCES

ARMED FORCES

The mission of the Armed Forces is to provide for the defense of our country by being prepared for war. The **Army** prepares for land-based defense, while the **Air Force** provides for air and space defense. The **Navy** organizes and trains forces primarily for sea defense. The **Marine Corps**, a branch of the Navy, prepares for land and sea actions in support of naval operations or amphibious landings. The **Coast Guard**, under the Department of Transportation (except in wartime, when it serves with the Navy), has responsibility for enforcing federal maritime laws, conducting rescues of distressed vessels and aircraft at sea, aids navigation, and prevents smuggling. Together, the military services constitute the largest employer in the country. They offer training opportunities and work experience in a wide range of occupational specialties, including managerial and administrative jobs, professional, technical, and clerical occupations, construction trades, electrical and electronic occupations, mechanic and repair occupations, and many others. The military provides job training and work experience for enlisted personnel, who typically enlist for 2 to 6 years, although some make a career of the military. Career opportunities are especially good for those in the officer corps. There are more than 2,000 basic and advanced military occupational specialties for enlisted personnel and 1,600 for officers. Many have civilian counterparts. Each of the military services publishes handbooks and pamphlets that describe entrance requirements, training and advancement opportunities, and other aspects of military careers. These publications are available at all recruiting stations, most state employment service offices, and in high schools, colleges, and public libraries.

U.S. ARMY RECRUITING COMMAND
Fort Sheridan, IL 60037

U.S. AIR FORCE RECRUITING SERVICE
Directorate of Advertising and Publicity
Randolph Air Force Base, TX 78150

U.S. MARINE CORPS
Personnel Procurement Division
Washington, DC 20380

NAVY OPPORTUNITY INFORMATION CENTER
P.O. Box 5000
Clifton, NJ 07015

U.S. COAST GUARD
Washington, DC 20593

ART

*Warning! Stay within the **industries** of this book. For example, commercial artist, medical publishing industry.*

COMMERCIAL ARTISTS

Commercial Artists design and create the artwork found on TV, brochures, records, product packages, greeting cards, and in newspapers and magazines. They must have creative instincts, professional training, and the ability to carry a project through from conception to completion. Many specialize in advertising art. Artists work for corporations in their art departments, for advertising companies, or are self-employed as free-lancers.

DESIGN INTERNATIONAL
3748 22d Street
San Francisco, CA 94114

DESIGN MANAGEMENT INSTITUTE
777 Boylston Street
Boston, MA 02116

GRAPHIC ARTS TECHNICAL FOUNDATION
4615 Forbes Avenue
Pittsburgh, PA 15213

SOCIETY OF ILLUSTRATORS
128 East 63rd Street
New York, NY 10021

AUCTIONEERING

AUCTIONEER

Sells articles at auction to highest bidder: Appraises merchandise before sale and assembles merchandise in lots according to estimated value of individual pieces or type of article. Selects article to be auctioned at suggestion of bidders or by own choice. Appraises article and determines or asks for starting bid. Describes merchandise and gives information about article, such as history and ownership, in order to encourage bidding. Continues to ask for bids, attempting to stimulate buying desire of bidders. Closes sale to highest bidder. May write auction catalog and advertising copy for local or trade newspapers and periodicals. May be designated according to property auctioned as AUCTIONEER, ART; AUCTIONEER, AUTOMOBILE; AUCTIONEER, FURNITURE; AUCTIONEER, LIVESTOCK; AUCTIONEER, REAL ESTATE; AUCTIONEER, TOBACCO.

LIVESTOCK MARKETING ASSOCIATION
301 East Armour Boulevard
Kansas City, MO 64111

NATIONAL AUCTIONEER'S ASSOCIATION
8880 Ballentine
Overland Park, KS 66214

NATIONAL AUTO AUCTION ASSOCIATION
57701 Russell Drive
P.O. Box 29100
Lincoln, NE 68529

BAIL BONDING

BONDING AGENT

Investigates arrested person to determine bondability: Interviews bond applicant to ascertain character and financial status. Furnishes bond for prescribed fee upon determining intention of accused to appear in court. Posts and signs bond with court clerk to obtain release of client. Forfeits amount of bond if client fails to appear for trial.

AMERICAN BAIL BONDSMAN ASSOCIATION
Lock Box 28185
Las Vegas, NV 89126

BROADCASTING

BROADCAST TECHNICIANS

Broadcast technicians operate and maintain the electronic equipment used to record and transmit radio and television programs. They work with microphones, sound and video tape recorders, light and sound effects, television cameras, transmitters, and other equipment. In the control room of the radio or television broadcasting studio, these technicians operate equipment that regulates the signal strength, clarity, and range of sounds and colors in the material being recorded or broadcast. They also operate control panels that select the source of the material being broadcast. Technicians may switch from one camera or studio to another, from film to live programming, or from network to local programs. They do this by means of hand signals and, in television, by use of telephone headsets. They give technical directions to personnel in the studio.

ASSOCIATION OF AUDIO-VISUAL TECHNICIANS
P.O. Box 9716
Denver, CO 80209

INTERNATIONAL SOCIETY OF CERTIFIED ELECTRONIC TECHNICIANS
2708 West Berry, Suite 8
Ft. Worth, TX 761009

NATIONAL ASSOCIATION OF TELEVISION ELECTRONICS SERVICERS OF AMERICA
4621 Kedzie Avenue
Chicago, IL 606625

RADIO AND TELEVISION ANNOUNCER

Announces radio and television programs to audience: Memorizes script, reads, or ad-libs to identify station, introduce and close shows, and announce station breaks, commercials, or public service information. Cues worker to transmit program from network central station or other pick-up points according to schedule. Reads news flashes to keep audience informed of important happenings. May rewrite news bulletin from wire service teletype to fit specific time slot. May describe public event such as parade or convention. May interview guest such as sport or other public personality and moderate panel or discussion show to entertain audience. May keep daily program log. In small stations may perform additional duties, such as operating control console or radio transmitter, selling time, or writing advertising copy. May announce in foreign language for international broadcast. May describe sporting event during game from direct observation or announce sports news received at station for radio or television broadcasting.

NATIONAL ASSOCIATION OF BROADCASTERS
1771 North Street, NW
Washington, DC 20036

NATIONAL BROADCAST EDITORIAL ASSOCIATION
6223 Executive Boulevard
Rockville, MD 20852

RADIO-TELEVISION NEWS DIRECTORS ASSOCIATION
1717 K Street, NW, Suite 615
Washington, DC 20006

CLEANING

JANITOR

Keeps hotel, office building, apartment house, or similar building in clean and orderly condition and tends furnace, air conditioner, and boiler to provide heat, cool air, and hot water for tenants, performing any combination of following duties: Sweeps and mops or scrubs hallways and stairs. Empties tenants' trash and garbage containers. Maintains building, performing minor and routine painting, plumbing, electrical wiring, and other related maintenance activities, using handtools. Replaces air conditioner filters. Cautions tenants regarding complaints about excessive noise, disorderly conduct, or misuse of property. Notifies management concerning need for major repairs or additions to lighting, heating, and ventilating equipment. Cleans snow and debris from sidewalk. Mows lawn, trims shrubbery, and cultivates flowers, using handtools and power tools. Posts signs to advertise vacancies and shows empty apartments to prospective tenants. May reside on property.

CLEANING & MANAGEMENT INSTITUTE
17911-C Skypark Boulevard
Irvine, CA 92714

CLERICAL

*Warning! Stay within the **industries** of this book. For example, legal secretary.*

SECRETARY

Schedules appointments, gives information to callers, takes dictation, and otherwise relieves officials of clerical work and minor administrative and business detail: Reads and routes incoming mail. Locates and attaches appropriate file to correspondence to be answered by employer. Takes dictation in shorthand or by machine and transcribes notes on typewriter, or transcribes from voice recordings. Composes and types routine correspondence. Files correspondence and other records. Answers telephone and gives information to callers or routes call to appropriate official and places outgoing calls. Schedules appointments for employer. Greets visitors, ascertains nature of business, and conducts visitors to employer or appropriate person. May take dictation. May arrange travel schedule and reservations. May compile and type statistical reports. May oversee clerical workers. May keep personnel records. May record minutes of staff meetings. May make copies of correspondence or other printed matter, using copying or duplicating machine. May prepare outgoing mail, using postage-metering machine.

SECRETARY, LEGAL

Prepares legal papers and correspondence of legal nature such as summonses, complaints, motions, and subpoenas. May review law journals and other legal publications to identify court decisions pertinent to pending cases and submit articles to company officials.

SECRETARY, MEDICAL

Performs secretarial duties utilizing knowledge of medical terminology and hospital, clinic, or laboratory procedures: Takes dictation in shorthand or using transcribing machine. Compiles and records medical charts, reports, and correspondence, using typewriter. May prepare and send bills to patients and record appointments.

SECRETARY, SCHOOL

Performs secretarial duties in elementary or secondary school: Composes own correspondence or transcribes correspondence, bulletins, and memorandum from rough draft, using typewriter. Receives and deposits funds for lunches, school supplies, and student activities. Disburses funds, records financial transactions, and audits and balances student-organization and other school-fund accounts. Maintains inventory of office and school supplies. May maintain calendar of school events. May procure assignments and texts for absent students for delivery to homes. May oversee student playground activities and monitor classroom during temporary absence of teacher. May check out and shelve books and collect fees and fines to assist librarian.

NATIONAL ASSOCIATION OF SECRETARIAL SERVICES
240 Driftwood Road, SE
St. Petersburg, FL 33705

PROFESSIONAL SECRETARIES INTERNATIONAL
301 East Armour Boulevard
Kansas City, MO 64111

CONSULTING

*Warning! Stay within the **industries** of this book. For example, insurance consultant.*

CONSULTANT

Consults with client to define need or problem. Conducts studies and surveys to obtain data, and analyzes data to advise on or recommend solution, utilizing knowledge of theory, principles, or technology of specific discipline or field of specialization: Consults with client to ascertain and define need or problem area, and determine scope of investigation required to obtain solution. Conducts study or survey on need or problem to obtain data required for solution. Analyzes data to determine solution, such as installation of alternate methods and procedures, changes in processing methods and practices, modification of machines or equipment, or redesign of products or services. Advises client on alternate methods of solving need or problem, or recommends specific solution. May negotiate contract for consulting service. May specialize in providing consulting service to government in field of specialization. May be designated according to field of specialization such as engineering or science discipline, economics, education, labor, or in specialized field of work as health services, social services, or investment services.

> **AMERICAN ASSOCIATION OF PROFESSIONAL CONSULTANTS**
> 9140 Ward Parkway
> Kansas City, MO 64114
>
> **AMERICAN CONSULTANTS LEAGUE**
> 2030 Clarendon Boulevard, Suite 202
> Arlington, VA 22201
>
> **PROFESSIONAL AND TECHNICAL CONSULTANTS ASSOCIATION**
> 1330 South Bascom Avenue, Suite D
> San Jose, CA 95128

CONSULTANT, COMPUTER

Computer systems analysts plan and develop methods for computerizing business and scientific tasks or for improving computer systems already in use. They may work for the organization that wants to install a system or for a consulting firm that develops systems under contract. Analysts begin an assignment by discussing the data processing problem with managers or specialists to determine the exact nature of the problem and to break it down into its component parts. After they have defined the goals of the system, they use techniques such as mathematical model building, sampling, and cost accounting to plan the system. Once a design for the system has been developed, systems analysts prepare charts and diagrams that describe it in terms that managers and other users can understand. They also may prepare a cost-benefit and return-on-investment analysis to help management decide whether proposed system is satisfactory. If the system is accepted, systems analysts may determine what computer hardware and software will be needed to set up the system. They also prepare specifications for programmers to follow and work with them to "debug" or eliminate errors from the system. The analyst also would design any forms required to collect data and distribute information. Because the possible uses for computers are so varied and complex, analysts usually specialize in either business, scientific, or engineering applications. Often, they have training or experience in the field in which they develop computer systems. Some analysts improve systems already in use by developing better procedures or adapting the system to handle additional types of data. Others do research, called advanced systems design, to devise new methods of systems analysis. A growing number of systems analysts are involved with connecting all the computers in an individual office, department, or establishment. This "networking" has many variations; they may be called local area networks, wide areas networks, or multiuser systems. A primary goal of networking is to allow users of micro-computers (also know as personal computers) to retrieve data from a mainframe computer and use it on their machine. This connection also allows data to be entered into the mainframe from the PC.

AMERICAN ASSOCIATION OF PROFESSIONAL CONSULTANTS
9140 Ward Parkway
Kansas City, MO 64114

AMERICAN CONSULTANTS LEAGUE
2030 Clarendon Boulevard, Suite 202
Arlington, VA 22201

PROFESSIONAL AND TECHNICAL CONSULTANTS ASSOCIATION
1330 South Bascom Avenue, Suite D
San Jose, CA 95128

CREDIT SERVICES

COLLECTOR
Notifies or locates customers of delinquent accounts and attempts to secure

payment, using postal services, telephone, or personal visit: Mails form letters to customers to encourage payment of delinquent accounts. Confers with customer by telephone in attempt to determine reason for overdue payment, reviewing terms of sales, service, or credit contract with customer. Prepares statements for credit department if customer fails to respond. May order repossession or service disconnection, or turn over account to attorney. May sort, read, answer, and file correspondence. May receive payments and post amount paid to customer's account. May grant extensions of credit. May void sales tickets for unclaimed C.O.D. and lay-away merchandise. May be designated according to type of establishment as BANK-CREDIT-CARD-COLLECTION CLERK; HOSPITAL-COLLECTION CLERK; UTILITY-BILL-COLLECTION CLERK. May personally interview or respond to correspondence or telephone inquiry from customers regarding delinquent bills, and whether any action taken is correct and whether adjustment of action taken is recommended. May trace customer to new address by inquiring at post office or by questioning neighbors. May attempt to repossess merchandise, such as automobile, furniture, and appliances when customer fails to make payment.

AMERICAN COLLECTORS ASSOCIATION, INC.
4040 West 70th Street
P.O. Box 35106
Minneapolis, MN 55435

CREDIT COUNSELOR

Provides financial counseling to individuals in debt: Confers with client to ascertain available monthly income after living expenses to meet credit obligations. Calculates amount of debt and funds available to plan method of payoff and estimate time for debt liquidation. Contacts creditors to explain client's financial situation and to arrange for payment adjustments so that payments are feasible for client and agreeable to creditors. Establishes payment priorities to reduce client's overall costs by liquidating high-interest, short-term loans or contracts first. Opens account for client and disburses funds from account to creditors as agent for client. Keeps records of account activity. May counsel client on personal and family financial problems, such as excessive spending and borrowing of funds. May be required to be licensed by state agency.

AMERICAN ASSOCIATION OF CREDIT COUNSELORS
P.O. Box 372
Graslake, IL 60030

INTERNATIONAL CREDIT ASSOCIATION
2243 North Lindbergh
P.O. Box 27357
St. Louis, MO 63141

NATIONAL ASSOCIATION OF CREDIT MANAGEMENT
520 Eighth Avenue
New York, NY 10018

REPOSSESSOR

Locates debtors and solicits payment for delinquent accounts and removes merchandise for nonpayment of account. May initiate repossession proceedings. May drive truck to return merchandise to creditor. May locate, enter, and start vehicle being repossessed, using special tools, if key cannot be obtained from debtor, and return vehicle to creditor. May be designated according to merchandise repossessed as AUTOMOBILE REPOSSESSOR.

AMERICAN RECOVERY ASSOCIATION
P.O. Box 6788
New Orleans, LA 70174

TOWING & RECOVERY ASSOCIATION OF AMERICA
P.O. Box 2517
Winter Park, FL 32790

DENTISTRY

DENTIST

Diagnoses and treats diseases, injuries, and malformations of teeth and gums, and related oral structures: Examines patient to determine nature of condition, utilizing X-rays, mouth mirrors, explorers, and other diagnostic procedures and instruments. Cleans, fills, extracts, and replaces teeth, using rotary and hand instruments, dental appliances, medications, and surgical implements.

AMERICAN ASSOCIATION OF DENTAL SCHOOLS
1625 Massachusetts Avenue, NW
Washington, DC 20036

AMERICAN DENTAL ASSOCIATION
211 East Chicago Avenue
Chicago, IL 60611

AMERICAN STUDENT DENTAL ASSOCIATION
211 East Chicago Avenue
Chicago, IL 60611

ENDODONTIST

Examines, diagnoses, and treats diseases of nerve, pulp, and other dental tissues affecting vitality of teeth: Examines teeth, gums, and related tissues to determine condition, using specific dental instruments, X-ray, and other diagnostic equipment. Diagnoses condition and plans treatment. Treats slight exposure of pulp by capping pulp chamber. Performs partial or total removal of pulp, using surgical instruments. Treats infected root canal and related tissues, and fills canal with specified material. Removes pathologic tissue, if indicated by surgery. Treats and reinserts or realigns teeth which have been lost or displaced. Bleaches discolored teeth to restore natural appearance.

AMERICAN ASSOCIATION OF ENDODONTISTS
211 East Chicago Avenue
Chicago, IL 60611

AMERICAN ENDODONTIC SOCIETY
1440 North Harbor Boulevard, Suite 719
Fullerton, CA 92635

HYGIENIST

Performs dental prophylaxis: Removes calcareous deposits, accretions, and stains from teeth by scaling accumulation of tartar from teeth and beneath margins of gums, using rotating brush, rubber cup, and cleaning compound. Applies medicaments to aid in arresting dental decay. Charts conditions of decay and disease for diagnosis and treatment by DENTIST. May expose and develop X-ray film. May make impressions for study casts. May remove sutures and dressings. May administer local anesthetic agents. May place and remove rubber dams, matrices, and temporary restorations. May place, carve, and finish amalgam restorations. May remove excess cement from coronal surfaces of teeth. May specialize in providing clinical services and health education in program designed to improve and maintain oral health of school children, in compliance with school policies and under direction of DENTIST and school administrator and be designated DENTAL HYGIENIST, PUBLIC SCHOOL. May specialize in lecturing community organizations and other interested groups on oral hygiene, using motion pictures, charts, and other visual aids, to augment service of PUBLIC-HEALTH DENTIST and be designated DENTAL HYGIENIST, COMMUNITY HEALTH.

AMERICAN DENTAL HYGIENISTS ASSOCIATION
444 North Michigan Avenue, Suite 3400
Chicago, IL 60611

NATIONAL ASSOCIATION OF DENTAL ASSISTANTS
3837 Plaza Drive
Fairfax, VA 22030

LABORATORY TECHNICIAN

Using their knowledge of dental anatomy and working from a dentist's prescription, dental lab technicians make dentures, fabricate metal or porcelain crowns and inlays, construct bridges, and make dental orthodontic appliances such as braces. The technician performs delicate and precise work using small hand-held instruments to produce an accurate fit and natural-looking effect. Most work in commercial laboratories. May own their own laboratories.

NATIONAL ASSOCIATION OF DENTAL LABORATORIES
3801 Mt. Vernon Avenue
Alexandria, VA 22305

ORAL PATHOLOGIST

Examines and diagnoses tumors and lesions of mouth: Examines specimens from patients' mouths to determine pathological conditions, using microscope and other laboratory equipment and applying knowledge of dentistry. Sends results of diagnosis to referring dental practitioner.

AMERICAN ACADEMY OF ORAL PATHOLOGISTS
c/o Dean K. White
Department of Oral Pathology
College of Dentistry
University of Kentucky
Lexington, KY 40536

AMERICAN BOARD OF ORAL PATHOLOGY
1121 West Michigan Street
Indiana University School of Dentistry
Indianapolis, IN 46202

ORAL SURGEON

Performs surgery on mouth and jaws: Executes difficult and multiple extraction of teeth. Removes tumors and other abnormal growths. Prepares mouth for insertion of dental prostheses by alveoloplasty and revision of oral soft tissues. Corrects abnormal jaw relations by mandibular or maxillary revision. Sets fractures of jaws. May treat patients in hospital.

AMERICAN ASSOCIATION OF ORAL & MAXILLOFACIAL SURGEONS
9700 West Bryn Mawr
Rosemont, IL 60018

ORTHODONTIST

Prevents, diagnoses, and corrects deviations from normal that occur in growth, development, and position of teeth and other dental-facial structures: Utilizes cephalometric and wrist radiograms, height and weight records, and front and lateral dental photographs in planning treatment. Designs intra- and extra-oral appliances to alter position and relationship of teeth and jaws to produce and maintain normal function. Fabricates appliances, such as space maintainers and regainers, bite planes, labial and lingual arch wires, and head caps.

AMERICAN ASSOCIATION OF ORTHODONTISTS
460 North Lindburg Boulevard
St. Louis, MO 63141

AMERICAN BOARD OF ORTHODONTICS
225 South Meramec Avenue
St. Louis, MO 63105

PERIODONTIST

Treats inflammatory and destructive diseases of investing and supporting tissue of teeth: Cleans and polishes teeth, eliminates irritating margins of fillings, and corrects occlusions. Performs gingivectomies, frenotomies, and flap operations, using prophylactic scalers and curettes, and osteoplasty and gingivoplasty instruments. Follows up treatment to insure maintenance of restored function and to determine that oral health practices are followed.

AMERICAN ACADEMY OF PERIODONTOLOGY
211 East Chicago Avenue, Suite 114
Chicago, IL 60611

PROSTHODONTIST

Restores and maintains oral functions: Records physiologic positions of jaws to determine shape and size of dental prostheses, using face bows, dental articulations, and other recording devices. Replaces missing teeth and associated oral structures with substitutes to improve mastication, speech, and appearance. Corrects natural and acquired deformation of mouth and jaws, using various appliances and instruments.

AMERICAN COLLEGE OF PROSTHODONTISTS
84 Northeast Loop 410, Suite 273 W
San Antonio, TX 78216

DIETETICS

DIETITIAN

Advises and assists personnel in public and private establishments, such as hospitals, health-related facilities, child-care centers, and schools, in food service systems and nutritional care of clients: Evaluates and monitors all aspects of food service operation, making recommendations for conformance level that will provide nutritionally adequate, quality food. Plans, organizes, and conducts orientation and in-service educational programs for food service personnel. Develops menu patterns. Assesses, develops, implements, and evaluates nutritional-care plans and provides for followup, including written reports. Consults with health care team concerning nutritional care of client. Confers with designers, builders, and equipment personnel in planning for building or remodeling food service units.

CONSULTANT DIETITIANS & HEALTH CARE FACILITIES
208 South LaSalle Street, Suite 1100
Chicago, IL 60604

EDUCATION

PRINCIPAL

Directs and coordinates educational, administrative, and counseling activities or primary or secondary school: Evaluates educational program to insure conformance to state and school board standards. Coordinates educational programs through meetings with staff, review of teaching department's activities, and issuance of directive. Confers with teaching personnel, pupils, and parents on matters pertaining to educational and behavioral problems in school. Establishes and maintains relationships with colleges, community organizations, and other schools to coordinate educational services. Requisitions and allocates supplies, equipment, and instructional material as needed. Supervises assignment of teachers and pupils to classes. May be designated PRINCIPAL, ELEMENTARY SCHOOL; PRINCIPAL, HIGH SCHOOL; PRINCIPAL, JUNIOR HIGH SCHOOL; PRINCIPAL, PRIVATE SCHOOL.

NATIONAL ASSOCIATION OF ELEMENTARY SCHOOL PRINCIPALS
1615 Duke Street
Alexandria, VA 22314

NATIONAL ASSOCIATION OF SECONDARY PRINCIPALS
1904 Association Drive
Reston, VA 22091

TEACHER, ACADEMIC

Teaches one or more subjects, such as English, mathematics, or social studies, to students in public or private secondary schools: Instructs students in subject matter utilizing various teaching methods, such as lecture and demonstration, and uses audiovisual aids and other materials to supplement presentations. Prepares teaching outline for course of study, assigns, lessons, and corrects homework papers. Administers tests to evaluate pupils' progress, records results, and issues reports to inform parents of progress. Keeps attendance records. Maintains discipline in classroom and school yard. Participates in faculty and professional meetings, educational conferences, and teacher training workshops. Performs related duties, such as sponsoring one or more special activities or student organizations, assisting pupils in selecting course of study, and counseling them in adjustment and academic problems. May be identified according to subject matter taught.

NATIONAL ASSOCIATION OF PROFESSIONAL EDUCATORS
412 First Street, SE
Washington, DC 20003

TEACHER, VOCATIONAL

Teaches vocational training subjects in specific trades to students in public or private schools or in industrial plants: Organizes program of practical and technical instruction, involving demonstrations of skills required in trade, and lectures on theory, practices, methods, processes, and terminology. Instructs students in subject areas, such as safety precautions, mathematics, science, drawing, use and maintenance of tools and equipment, and codes or regulations related to trade. Plans and supervises work of students in shop or laboratory. Tests and evaluates achievement of student in technical knowledge and trade skills. May be identified according to trade or theory taught or type of establishment in which training is conducted.

NATIONAL ASSOCIATION OF PROFESSIONAL EDUCATORS
412 First Street, SE
Washington, DC 20003

FIRE-PROTECTION ENGINEER

Advises and assists private and public organizations and military services for purposes of safeguarding life and property against fire, explosion, and related hazards: Makes studies of industrial, mercantile, and public buildings, homes, and other property before and after construction, considering factors, such as fire resistance of construction, usage or contents of buildings, water supplies and water delivery, and egress facilities. Designs or recommends materials or equipment, such as structural components protection, fire-detection equipment, alarm systems, fire extinguishing devices and systems, and advises on location, handling, installation, and maintenance. Recommends materials, equipment, or methods for alleviation of conditions conducive to fire. Devises fire protection programs, organizes and trains personnel to carry out such programs. May evaluate fire departments and adequacy of laws, ordinances, and regulations affecting fire prevention or fire safety. Conducts research and tests on fire retardants and fire safety of materials and devices. May determine fire causes and methods of fire prevention. May teach courses on fire prevention and protection at accredited educational institutions. May advise and plan for prevention of destruction by fire, wind, water, or other causes of damage.

NATIONAL FIRE PROTECTION ASSOCIATION
Battery March Park
Quincy, MA 02269

SOCIETY OF FIRE PROTECTION ENGINEERS
60 Battery March Street
Boston, MA 02110

SOCIETY OF FIRE PROTECTION TECHNICIANS
29 Oriole Drive
West Trenton, NJ 08628

SAFETY ENGINEER

Develops and implements safety program to prevent or correct unsafe environmental working conditions, utilizing knowledge of industrial processes, mechanics, chemistry, psychology, and industrial health and safety laws: Examines plans and specifications for new machinery and equipment to ascertain if all safety precautions have been included. Determines amount of weight that can be placed on plant floor with safety. Inspects machinery to determine places where danger of injury exists. Designs, builds, and installs or directs installation of guards on machinery, belts, and conveyors. Inspects premises for fire hazards and adequacy of fire protection and inspects firefighting equipment. Studies each accident to minimize recurrence. Educates workers to dangers existing in plant through safety-first campaign. May conduct safety and first-aid classes or train first-aid instructors.

AMERICAN SOCIETY OF SAFETY ENGINEERS
1800 East Oakton Street
Des Plaines, IL 60016

SANITARY ENGINEER

Designs and directs construction and operation of hygienic projects such as waterworks, sewage, garbage and trash disposal plants, drainage systems, and insect and rodent control projects: Plans development of watersheds and directs building of aqueducts, filtration plants, and storage and distribution systems for water supply. Directs swamp drainage, insect spraying, and design of insect-proof buildings. Plans and directs workers in building and operation of sewage-disposal plants. Designs and controls operation of incinerators, sanitary fills, and garbage-reduction plants to dispose of garbage and other refuse. Advises industrial plants in disposal of obnoxious gases, oils, greases, and other chemicals. Inspects and regulates sanitary condition of public places, such as markets, parks, and camps. May plan and direct operation of water treatment plant to soften and purify water for human consumption or industrial use and be know as WATER-TREATMENT-PLANT ENGINEER.

AMERICAN SOCIETY OF SANITARY ENGINEERING
P.O. Box 40362
Bay Village, OH 44140

INTER-AMERICAN ASSOCIATION OF SANITARY ENGINEERING ENVIRONMENTAL SCIENCES
18729 Considine Drive
Brookeville, MD 20833

FIRE FIGHTING

FIRE FIGHTER

Controls and extinguishes fires, protects life and property, and maintains equipment as volunteer or employee of city, township, or industrial plant: Responds to fire alarms and other emergency calls. Selects hose nozzle, depending on type of fire, and directs stream of water or chemicals onto fire. Positions and climbs ladders to gain access to upper levels of buildings to assist individuals from burning structures. Creates openings in buildings for ventilation or entrance, using ax, chisel, crowbar, electric saw, core cutter, and other power equipment. Protects property from water and smoke by use of waterproof salvage covers, smoke ejectors, and deodorants. Administers first aid and artificial respiration to injured persons and those overcome by fire and smoke. Communicates with superior during fire, using portable two-way radio. Inspects buildings for fire hazards and compliance with fire prevention ordinances. Performs assigned duties in maintaining apparatus, quarters, buildings equipment, grounds, and hydrants. Participates in drills, demonstrations, and courses in hydraulics, pump operation and maintenance, and firefighting techniques. May fill fire extinguishers in institutions or industrial plants. May issue forms to building owners listing fire regulation violations to be corrected. May drive and operate firefighting vehicles and equipment. May be assigned duty in marine division of fire department and be designated FIREFIGHTER, MARINE.

INTERNATIONAL ASSOCIATION OF FIREFIGHTERS
1750 New York Avenue, NW
Washington, DC 20006

INTERNATIONAL FIRE SERVICE TRAINING ASSOCIATION
Fire Protection Publications
Oklahoma State University
Stillwater, OK 74078

INTERNATIONAL SOCIETY OF FIRE SERVICE INSTRUCTORS
20 Main Street
Ashland, MA 01721

FIRE INSPECTOR

Inspects premises of industrial plant to detect and eliminate fire hazards: Inspects fire-extinguishing and fire-protection equipment to insure equipment is operable and prepares reports listing repairs and replacements needed. Patrols plant areas and notes and investigates unsafe conditions and practices which might cause or increase fire hazards. Reports findings to FIRE MARSHAL with recommendations for eliminating or counteracting hazards. Renders first aid in emergencies. Patrols plant areas in which raw and combustible materials are stored, takes temperature and pressure readings from instruments, and reports undesirable conditions or takes steps to correct such conditions. May instruct employees in fire safety practices. May perform tests on fire-prevention equipment in plants where explosive or flammable materials are processed. May participate in fighting fires.

NATIONAL ASSOCIATION OF FIRE INVESTIGATORS
20 East Jackson, Suite 1000
Chicago, IL 60604

FIRE MARSHAL (INDUSTRIAL)

Supervises and coordinates activities of firefighting personnel of industrial establishment and inspects equipment and premises to insure adherence to fire regulations: Inspects and orders replacement or servicing of firefighting equipment, such as sprinklers and extinguishers. Issues permits for storage and use of hazardous or flammable materials. Inspects premises to detect combustion hazards. Orders and directs fire drills. Directs firefighting and rescue activities according to knowledge of accepted procedures. May be designated according to employing establishment.

FIRE MARSHALS ASSOCIATION OF NORTH AMERICA
1110 Vermont Avenue, NW, Suite 1210
Washington, DC 20005

FIRE MARSHAL (GOV.)

Investigates and gathers facts to determine cause of fires and explosions and enforces fire laws: Investigates case when (1) arson or criminal negligence is suspected; (2) multialarm fire results in serious injury or death; or (3) fire takes place in commercial establishment of public building. Examines fire site to determine burn pattern and detect presence of flammable materials and gases and incendiary devices, using various detectors. Performs match test to determine flash point of suspicious material at fire site. Subpoenas and interviews witnesses, building owners, and occupants to obtain sworn testimony of observed facts. Prepares reports on each investigation and submits data indicating arson to district attorney. Arrests, logs fingerprints, and detains arson suspect. Testifies in court, citing evidence obtained from investigation. Conducts inquiries into departmental employees delinquency in performance of duties and violation of laws or regulations.

FIRE MARSHALS ASSOCIATION OF NORTH AMERICA
1110 Vermont Avenue, NW, Suite 1210
Washington, DC 20005

INTERNATIONAL ASSOCIATION OF ARSON INVESTIGATORS
5428 Del Maria Way #201
P.O. Box 91119
Louisville, KY 40291

FUNDRAISING

FUNDRAISER

Plans fund raising program for charities or other causes. Compiles and analyzes information about potential contributors to develop mailing or contact list and to plan selling approach. Writes, telephones, or visits potential contributors and persuades them to contribute funds by explaining purpose and benefits of fund raising program. Takes pledges or funds from contributors. Records expenses incurred and contributions received. May organize volunteers and plan social functions to raise funds. May prepare fund raising brochures for mail solicitation programs.

NATIONAL ASSOCIATION OF PROFESSIONAL FUND RAISERS
501 West Algonquin Road
Arlington Heights, IL 60005

NATIONAL SOCIETY OF FUND RAISING EXECUTIVES
1101 King Street, Suite 3000
Alexandria, VA 22314

FUNERAL SERVICES

EMBALMER
Prepares bodies for interment in conformity with legal requirements: Washes and dries body, using germicidal soap and towels or hot air drier. Inserts convex celluloid or cotton between eyeball and eyelid to prevent slipping and sinking of eyelid. Presses diaphragm to evacuate air from lungs. May join lips, using needle land thread or wire. Packs body orifices with cotton saturated with embalming fluid to prevent escape of gases or waste matter. Makes incision in arm or thigh, using scalpel, inserts pump tubes into artery, and starts pump that drains blood from circulatory system and replaces blood with embalming fluid. Incises stomach and abdominal walls and probes internal organs, such as bladder and liver, using trocar to withdraw blood and waste matter from organs. Attaches trocar to pump-tube, starts pump, and repeats probing to force embalming fluid into organs. Closes incisions, using needle and suture. Reshapes or reconstructs disfigured or maimed bodies, using materials, such as clay, cotton, plaster of paris, and wax. Applies cosmetics to impart lifelike appearance. Dresses body and places body in casket. May arrange funeral details, such as type of casket or burial dress and place of interment. May maintain records, such as itemized list of clothing or valuables delivered with body and names of persons embalmed.

AMERICAN BOARD OF FUNERAL SERVICE EDUCATION
23 Crestwood Road
Cumberland, ME 04021

NATIONAL SELECTED MORTICIANS
1616 Central Street
Evanston, IL 60210

FUNERAL DIRECTOR

Arranges and directs funeral services: Coordinates activities of workers to remove body to mortuary for embalming. Interviews family or other authorized person to arrange details, such as preparation of obituary notice, selection of urn or casket, determination of location and time of cremation or burial, selection of pallbearers, procurement of official for religious rites, and transportation of mourners. Plans placement of casket in parlor or chapel and adjusts lights, fixtures, and floral displays. Directs pallbearers in placement and removal of casket from hearse. Closes casket and leads funeral cortege to church or burial site. Directs preparations and shipment of body for out of state burial. May prepare body for interment.

AMERICAN BOARD OF FUNERAL SERVICE EDUCATION
23 Crestwood Road
Cumberland, ME 04021

ASSOCIATED FUNERAL DIRECTORS SERVICE INTERNATIONAL
P.O. Box 7476
810 Stratford Avenue
Tampa, FL 33603

CONTINENTAL ASSOCIATION OF FUNERAL & MEMORIAL SOCIETIES
2001 South Street, NW, Suite 530
Washington, DC 20009

CREMATION ASSOCIATION OF NORTH AMERICA
111 East Wacker Drive, Suite 600
Chicago, IL 60601

NATIONAL FUNERAL DIRECTORS ASSOCIATION
135 West Wells Street, Suite 600
Milwaukee, WI 53203

NATIONAL FUNERAL DIRECTORS & MORTICIANS ASSOCIATION
5723 South Indiana Avenue
Chicago, IL 60637

NATIONAL SELECTED MORTICIANS
1616 Central Street
Evanston, IL 60210

TELOPHASE SOCIETY (MORTUARY SERVICES & BURIAL AT SEA)
1333 Camino Del Rio South
San Diego, CA 92108

MORTUARY BEAUTICIAN

Prepares embalmed female bodies for interment: Manicures nails, using files and nail polish, and performs other grooming tasks, such as arching and plucking eyebrows and removing facial hair, using depilatory cream and tweezers. Shampoos, waves, presses, curls, brushes, and combs hair, and applies cosmetics on face to restore natural appearance, following photograph of deceased, or verbal or written description obtained from family. Dresses and arranges body in casket. May select casket or burial dress, arrange floral displays, and prepare obituary notices. May record personal effects delivered with body and information about deceased. May wash and dry bodies, using germicidal soap and towels or hot air drier. May reshape or reconstruct damaged or disfigured areas of body, using such materials as cotton or foam rubber.

AMERICAN BOARD OF FUNERAL SERVICE EDUCATION
23 Crestwood Road
Cumberland, ME 04021

NATIONAL SELECTED MORTICIANS
1616 Central Street
Evanston, IL 60210

HAIRSTYLING

BARBER
Provides customers with barbering services: Cuts, blows, trims, and tapers hair, using clippers, comb, blow gun, and scissors. Applies lather and shaves beard or shapes hair contour (outline) on temple and neck, using razor. Performs other tonsorial services, such as applying hairdressings or lotions, dyeing, shampooing, singeing, or styling hair, and massaging face, neck, or scalp. Records service charge on ticket. May sell lotions, tonics, or other cosmetic supplies.

NATIONAL ASSOCIATION OF BARBER BOARDS
65 South Front Street, Suite 306
Columbus, OH 43215

HAIR INTERNATIONAL/ASSOCIATED MASTER BARBERS & BEAUTICIANS OF AMERICA
219 Greenwich Road
Charlotte, NC 28211

NATIONAL ASSOCIATION OF BARBER STYLING SCHOOLS
304 South 11th Street
Lincoln, NE 68508

NATIONAL BARBER CAREER CENTER
3839 White Plains Road
Bronx, NY 10467

COSMETOLOGIST
Provides beauty services for customers: Analyzes hair to ascertain condition of

hair. Applies bleach, dye, or tint, using applicator or brush, to color customer's hair. Shampoos hair and scalp with water, liquid soap, dry powder, or egg, and rinses hair with vinegar, water, lemon, or prepared rinses. Massages scalp and gives other hair and scalp conditioning treatments for hygienic or remedial purposes. Styles hair by blowing, cutting, trimming, and tapering, using clippers, scissors, razors, and blow-wave gun. Suggests coiffure according to physical features of patron and current styles, or determines coiffure from instructions of patron. Applies water or waving solutions to hair and winds hair around rollers, or pin curls and finger-waves hair. Sets hair by blow-dry or natural-set, or presses hair with straightening comb. Suggests cosmetics for conditions, such as dry or oily skin. Applies lotions and creams to customer's face and neck to soften skin and lubricate tissues. Performs other beauty services, such as massaging face or neck, shaping and coloring eyebrows or eyelashes, removing unwanted hair, applying solutions that straighten hair or retain curls or waves in hair, and waving or curling hair. Cleans, shapes and polishes fingernails and toenails.

AMERICAN COUNCIL ON COSMETOLOGY EDUCATION & NATIONAL ASSOCIATION OF COSMETOLOGY SCHOOLS
1990 M Street, NW, Suite 650
Washington, DC 20036

ASSOCIATION OF COSMETOLOGISTS
1811 Monroe
Dearborne, MI 48124

INTERNATIONAL CHAIN SALON ASSOCIATION
101 East Ontario Street
Frankfort, IL 60423

NATIONAL HAIRDRESSERS & COSMETOLOGISTS ASSOCIATION
3510 Olive Street
St. Louis, MO 63103

NATIONAL AESTHETICIAN & NAIL ARTIST ASSOCIATION
16 North Wabash Avenue, Suite 1212
Chicago, IL 60602

INSURANCE

ACTUARY

Applies knowledge of mathematics, probability, statistics, principles of finance and business to problems in life, health, social, and casualty insurance, annuities, and pensions: Determines mortality, accident, sickness, disability, and retirement rates; constructs probability tables regarding fire, natural disasters, and unemployment, based on analysis of statistical data and other pertinent information.

Designs or reviews insurance and pension plans and calculates premiums. Ascertains premium rates required and cash reserves and liabilities necessary to insure payment of future benefits. Determines equitable basis for distributing surplus earnings under participating insurance and annuity contracts in mutual companies. May specialize in one type of insurance and be designated as ACTUARY, CASUALTY; ACTUARY, LIFE.

CASUALTY ACTUARIAL SOCIETY
One Penn Plaza
250 West 34th Street, 51st Floor
New York, NY 10119

SOCIETY OF ACTUARIES
500 Park Boulevard
Itasca, IL 60143

APPRAISER, AUTOMOBILE DAMAGE

Appraises automobile or other vehicle damage to determine cost of repair for insurance claim settlement and attempts to secure agreement with automobile repair shop on cost of repair: Examines damaged vehicle to determine extent of structural, body, mechanical, electrical, or interior damage. Estimates cost of labor and parts to repair or replace each item of damage, using standard automotive labor and parts cost manuals and knowledge of automotive repair. Determines salvage value on total-loss vehicle. Evaluates practicality of repair as opposed to payment of market value of vehicle before accident. Prepares insurance forms to indicate repair-cost estimates and recommendations. Reviews repair-cost estimates with automobile repair shop to secure agreement on cost of repairs. Occasionally arranges to have damage appraised by another appraiser to resolve disagreement with repair shop on repair cost.

INDEPENDENT AUTO DAMAGE APPRAISERS
P.O. Box 1447
Boynton Beach, FL 33435

BUILDING INSPECTOR

Inspects buildings to determine fire insurance rates: Examines building for type of construction, condition of roof, and fireproofing. Determines risk represented by adjoining buildings, by nature of business, and building contents. Determines availability of fireplugs and firefighting equipment. Completes inspection report. May compute insurance rate.

INSURANCE INFORMATION INSTITUTE
110 William Street
New York, NY 10038

CLAIM ADJUSTER

Investigates claims against insurance or other companies for personal, casualty, or property loss or damages and attempts to effect out-of-court settlement with claimant: Examines claim form and other records to determine insurance coverage. Interviews, telephones, or corresponds with claimant and witnesses; consults police and hospital records; and inspects property damage to determine extent of company's liability, varying method of investigation according to type of insurance. Prepares report of findings and negotiates settlement with claimant. Recommends litigation by legal department when settlement cannot be negotiated. May attend litigation hearings. May be designated according to type of claim adjusted as AUTOMOBILE-INSURANCE-CLAIM ADJUSTER; CASUALTY-INSUR-ANCE-CLAIM ADJUSTER; FIDELITY-AND-SURETY-BONDS-CLAIM ADJUSTER; FIRE-INSURANCE-CLAIM ADJUSTER; MARINE-INSURANCE-CLAIM ADJUSTER; PROPERTY-LOSS-INSURANCE-CLAIM ADJUSTER.

ALLIANCE OF AMERICAN INSURERS
1501 Woodfield Road, Suite 400 W
Schaumburg, IL 60195

INTERNATIONAL CLAIM ASSOCIATION
c/o Modern Woodman of America
1701 First Avenue
Rock Island, IL 61202

NATIONAL ASSOCIATION OF INDEPENDENT INSURANCE ADJUSTERS
222 West Adams Street
Chicago, IL 60606

CLAIM EXAMINER

Analyzes insurance claims to determine extent of insurance carrier's liability and settles claims with claimants in accordance with policy provisions: Compares data on claim application, death certificate, or physician's statement with policy file and other company records to ascertain completeness and validity of claim. Corresponds with agents and claimants or interviews them in person to correct errors or omissions on claim forms, and to investigate questionable entries. Pays claimant amount due. Refers most questionable claims to INVESTIGATOR or to CLAIM ADJUSTER for investigation and settlement. May investigate claims in field. May be designated according to type of claim handled as ACCIDENT-AND-HEALTH INSURANCE-CLAIM EXAMINER; AUTOMOBILE-INSURANCE-CLAIM

EXAMINER; DEATH-CLAIM EXAMINER; DISABILITY-INSURANCE-CLAIM EX-
AMINER; FIRE-INSURANCE-CLAIM EXAMINER; MARINE-INSURANCE-CLAIM
EXAMINER.

ALLIANCE OF AMERICAN INSURERS
1501 Woodfield Road, Suite 400 W
Schaumburg, IL 60195

INTERNATIONAL CLAIM ASSOCIATION
c/o Modern Woodman of America
1701 First Avenue
Rock Island, IL 61202

NATIONAL ASSOCIATION OF INDEPENDENT INSURANCE ADJUSTERS
222 West Adams Street
Chicago, IL 60606

RESEARCH ANALYST

Evaluates insurance industry developments to update company products and
procedures: Reviews industry publications and monitors pending legislation and
regulations to determine impact of new developments on company insurance
products. Consults with designated company personnel to disseminate information necessitating changes in language or provisions of insurance contracts and
assists in preparation of documents or directives needed to implement changes.
Corresponds or consults with agents, brokers, and other interested persons to
determine feasibility and marketability of new products to meet competition and
increase sales. Develops procedures and materials for introduction and administration of new products, and submits package for review by company personnel
and regulatory bodies. May recommend lobbying activities to management. May
direct or coordinate activities of other workers. May specialize in analyzing
developments in group insurance operations and be designated GROUP CON-
TRACT ANALYST.

INSURANCE INFORMATION INSTITUTE
110 William Street
New York, NY 10038

SAFETY INSPECTOR

Inspects insured properties to evaluate physical conditions and promote safety
programs: Inspects properties such as buildings, industrial operations, vehicles,
and recreational facilities to evaluate physical conditions, safety practices, and
hazardous situations according to knowledge of safety and casualty underwriting
standards and governmental regulations. Measures insured area, calculates

frontage, and records description and amount of stock, and photographs or drafts scale drawings of properties to identify factors affecting insurance premiums. Analyzes history of accidents and claims against insured and inspects scenes of accidents to determine causes and to develop accident-prevention programs. Prepares written report of findings and recommendations for correction of unsafe or unsanitary conditions. Confers with employees of insured to induce compliance with safety standards, codes, and regulations. Conducts informational meetings among various educational, civic, and industrial groups, to promote general safety concepts, utilizing, audiovisual aids and insurance statistics. May specialize in specific type of accident-prevention or safety program, such as fire safety or traffic safety.

INSURANCE INFORMATION INSTITUTE
110 William Street
New York, NY 10038

SALES AGENT (SEE SALES)

UNDERWRITER

Reviews individual applications for insurance to evaluate degree of risk involved and accepts applications, following company's underwriting policies: Examines such documents as application form, inspection report, insurance maps, and medical reports to determine degree of risk from such factors as applicant's financial standing, age, occupation, accident experience, and value and condition of real property. Reviews company records to ascertain amount of insurance in force on single risk or group of closely related risks, and evaluates possibility of losses due to catastrophe or excessive insurance. Declines risks which are too excessive to obligate company. Dictates correspondence for field representatives, medical personnel, and other insurance or inspection companies to obtain further information, quote rates, or explain company's underwriting policies. When risk is excessive, authorizes reinsurance, or when risk is substandard, limits company's obligation by decreasing value of policy, specifying applicable endorsements, or applying rating to insure safe and profitable distribution of risks, using rate books, tables, code books, and other reference material. Typically, workers who under-write one type of insurance do not underwrite others, and are designated according to type of insurance underwritten as ACCIDENT-AND-SICKNESS UNDERWRITER; AUTOMOBILE UNDERWRITER; BOND UNDERWRITER; CASUALTY UNDER-WRITER; COMPENSATION UNDERWRITER; CREDIT-LIFE UNDERWRITER; FIRE UNDERWRITER; GROUP UNDERWRITER; LIABILITY UNDERWRITER; LIFE UNDERWRITER; MARINE UNDERWRITER; MULTIPLE-LINE UNDERWRITER; PENSION-AND-ADVANCED UNDERWRITING SPECIALIST; REINSTATEMENT

UNDERWRITER; SPECIAL-RISKS UNDERWRITER. When underwriting group policies solely on basis of medical examinations, may be designated as MEDICAL-STATEMENT APPROVER.

INSTITUTE OF HOME OFFICE UNDERWRITERS
c/o James R. Fagan
Commonwealth Life Insurance Company
Fourth and Broadway
Louisville, KY 40202

JOURNALISM

PHOTOJOURNALIST

Photographs newsworthy events, locations, people, or other illustrative or educational material for use in publications or telecasts: Travels to assigned location and takes pictures. Develops negatives and prints film. Submits negatives and pictures to editorial personnel. Usually specializes in one phase of photography, as news, sports, special features, or as a free-lance photographer.

NATIONAL FREE-LANCE PHOTOGRAPHERS ASSOCIATION
Ten South Pine Street
Box 629
Doyleston, PA 18901

NATIONAL PRESS PHOTOGRAPHERS ASSOCIATION
3200 Croasdaile Drive, Suite 306
Durham, NC 27705

REPORTER

Collects and analyzes information about newsworthy events to write news stories for publication or broadcast: Receives assignment or evaluates leads and news tips to develop story idea. Gathers and verifies factual information regarding story through interview, observation, and research. Organizes material, determines slant or emphasis, and writes story according to prescribed editorial style and format standards. May monitor police and fire department radio communications to obtain story leads. May take photographs to illustrate stories. May appear on television program when conducting taped or filmed interviews or narration. May give live reports from site of event or mobile broadcast unit. May transmit information to NEWSWRITER for story writing. May specialize in one type of reporting, such as sports, fires, accidents, political affairs, court trials, or police activities. May be assigned to outlying areas or foreign countries and be designated CORRESPONDENT or FOREIGN CORRESPONDENT.

ACCREDITING COUNCIL ON EDUCATION IN JOURNALISM AND MASS COMMUNICATIONS
School of Journalism
University of Kansas
Lawrence, KS 66045

AMERICAN NEWSPAPER PUBLISHERS ASSOCIATION
The Newspaper Center
Box 17407, Dulles International Airport
Washington, DC 20041

THE NEWSPAPER GUILD
Research and Information Department
1125 15th Street, NW
Washington, DC 20005

LAW AND JURISPRUDENCE

COURT REPORTER

Records examination, testimony, judicial opinions, judge's charge to jury, judgement, or sentence of court, or other proceedings in court of law by machine shorthand. Reads portions of transcript during trial on judge's request, and asks speakers to clarify inaudible statements. Operates typewriter to transcribe recorded material, or dictates material into recording machine. May record proceedings of quasi-judicial hearings, formal and informal meetings, and be designated HEARINGS REPORTER. May be self-employed, performing duties in court of law or at hearings and meetings, and be designated FREE-LANCE REPORTER.

NATIONAL SHORTHAND REPORTERS ASSOCIATION
118 Park Street, SE
Vienna, VA 22180

LAWYER

Lawyers act as both advocates and advisors. As advocates, they represent one of the opposing parties in criminal and civil trials by presenting arguments that support the client in a court of law. As advisors, lawyers counsel their clients as to their legal rights and obligations and suggest particular courses of action in business and personal matters. Whether acting as advocates or advisors, nearly all attorneys have certain activities in common. Probably the most fundamental activities are the interpretation of the law and its application to a specific situation. This requires in-depth research into the purposes behind the applicable laws and into judicial decisions that have applied those laws to circumstances similar to those currently faced by the client. Based on this research, attorneys advise clients on what actions would best serve their interests. A few lawyers specialize in trial work. These lawyers need an exceptional ability to think quickly and speak with ease and authority, and must be thoroughly familiar with courtroom rules and strategy. Trial lawyers still spend most of their time outside the courtroom conducting research, interviewing clients and witnesses, and handling other details in preparation for trial. Although most lawyers deal with many different areas of the law, a significant number concentrate on one branch of law, such as admiralty, probate, or international law. Communications lawyers, for example, may represent radio and television stations in court and in their dealings with the Federal Communications Commission. They help established stations prepare and file license renewal applications, employment reports, and other documents required by the FCC on a regular basis. They also keep their clients informed of changes in FCC regulations. Communications lawyers help individuals or corporations buy or sell a station or establish a new one. Lawyers who represent public utilities before the Federal Energy Regulatory Commission and other federal and state regulatory agencies handle matters involving utility rates. They develop strategy, arguments, and testimony; prepare cases for presentation; and argue the case. These lawyers also inform clients about changes in regulations and give advice about the legality of their actions. Still other lawyers advise insurance companies about the legality of insurance transactions. They write insurance policies to conform with the law and to protect companies from unwarranted claims. They review claims filed against insurance companies and represent companies in court. Lawyers in private practice may concentrate on areas such as litigation, wills, trusts, contract, mortgages, titles, and leases. Some manage a person's property as trustee or, as executor, see that provisions of a client's will are carried out. Others handle only public interest cases-civil or criminal-which have a potential impact extending well beyond the individual client. Attorneys hope to use these cases as a vehicle for legal and social reform. A lawyer may be employed full time by a single client. If the client is a corporation, the lawyer is known as house counsel and usually advises a company about legal questions that arise from its business activities. These questions might involve patents, government regulations, a business contract with another company, a property interest, or a collective bargaining agreement with a union. Attorneys employed at the various levels of government constitute still another category. Criminal lawyers may work for a state attorney general, a prosecutor or public defender, or a court. At the federal level, attorneys may investigate cases for the Department of Justice or other agencies. Lawyers at every government level help develop laws and programs, draft and interpret legislation, establish enforcement procedures, and argue cases. Other lawyers work for legal aid societies. These lawyers generally handle civil rather then criminal cases. A relatively small number of trained attorneys work in law schools. Most are faculty members who specialize in one or more subjects, while others serve as administrators. Some work full time in nonacademic settings and teach part time.

AMERICAN ASSOCIATION OF ATTORNEY-CERTIFIED PUBLIC ACCOUNTANTS
24001 Alicia Parkway, Suite 101
Mission Viejo, CA 92691

AMERICAN LAWYERS AUXILIARY
c/o Sheri L. Heald
750 North Lakeshore Drive
Chicago, IL 60611

NATIONAL BAR ASSOCIATION
1225 11th Street, NW
Washington, DC 20001

PARALEGAL

Researches law, investigates facts, and prepares documents to assist LAWYER: Researches and analyzes law sources such as statutes, recorded judicial decisions, legal articles, treaties, constitutions, and legal codes to prepare legal documents such as briefs, pleadings, appeals, wills, contracts, deeds, and trust instruments for review, approval, and use by attorney. Appraises and inventories real and personal property for estate planning. Investigates facts and law of case to determine causes of action and to prepare case accordingly. Files pleadings with court clerk. Prepares affidavits of documents and maintains document file. Delivers or directs delivery of subpoenas to witnesses and parties to action. May direct and coordinate activities of law office employees. May prepare office accounts and tax returns. May specialize in litigation, probate, real estate, or corporate law. May search patent files to ascertain originality of patent application and be designated PATENT CLERK.

INSTITUTE FOR PARALEGAL TRAINING
1926 Arch Street
Philadelphia, PA 19103

NATIONAL ASSOCIATION OF LEGAL ASSISTANTS
1601 South Main Street, Suite 300
Tulsa, OK 74119

NATIONAL FEDERATION OF PARALEGAL ASSOCIATIONS
104 Wilmot Road, Suite 201
Deerfield, IL 60015

PROCESS SERVER

Serves court orders and processes, such as summonses and subpoenas: Receives papers to be served from magistrate, court clerk, or attorney. Locates person to be served, using telephone directories, state, county, and city records, or public utility records, and delivers document. Records time and place of delivery. May deliver general messages and documents between courts and attorneys.

LAW ENFORCEMENT

CORONER

Directs investigation of deaths occurring within jurisdiction as required by law: Directs activities of staff physicians, technicians, and investigators involved with conducting inquests, performing autopsies, conducting pathological and toxicological analyses, and investigating circumstances of deaths in order to determine cause and fix responsibility for accidental, violent, or unexplained deaths, or contracts for such services with outside physicians, medical laboratories, and law enforcement agencies. Testifies at inquests, hearings, and court trials. Confers with officials of public health and law enforcement agencies to coordinate interdepartmental activities. Coordinates activities for disposition of unclaimed corpse and personal effects of deceased. Directs activities of workers involved in preparing documents for permanent records. May assist relatives of deceased in negotiations concerning payment of insurance policies or burial benefits by providing information concerning circumstances of death. May be required by law or ordinance to have specified medical or legal training.

CORRECTION OFFICER

Guards inmates in penal institution in accordance with established policies, regulations, and procedures: Observes conduct and behavior of inmates to prevent disturbances and escapes. Inspects locks, window bars, grills, doors, and gates for tampering. Searches inmates and cells for contraband articles. Guards and directs inmates during work assignments. Patrols assigned areas for evidence of forbidden activities, infraction of rules and unsatisfactory attitudes or adjustment of prisoners. Reports observations to superior. Employs weapons or force to maintain discipline and order among prisoners, if necessary. May escort inmates to and from visiting room, medical office, and religious services. May guard entrance of jail to screen visitors. May prepare written report concerning incidences of inmate disturbances or injuries. May be designated according to institution as CORRECTION OFFICER, CITY OR COUNTY JAIL; CORRECTION OFFICER, PENITENTIARY; CORRECTION OFFICER, REFORMATORY. May guard prisoners in transit between jail, courtroom, prison, or other point, traveling by automobile or public transportation, and be designated GUARD, DEPUTY

INTERNATIONAL ASSOCIATION OF CORRECTIONAL OFFICERS
c/o Robert Barrington
P.O. Box 7051
Marquette, MI 49855

CRIMINALIST

Applies scientific principles to analysis, identification, and classification of mechanical devices, chemical and physical substances, materials, liquids, or other physical evidence related to criminology, law enforcement, or investigative work: Searches for, collects, photographs, and preserves evidence. Performs variety of analytical examinations, utilizing chemistry, physics, mechanics, and other sciences. Analyzes items, such as paint, glass, printed matter, paper, ink, fabric, dust, dirt, gases, or other substances, using spectroscope, microscope, infrared and ultraviolet light, microphotography, gas chromatograph, or other recording, measuring, or testing instruments. Identifies hair, skin, tissue, blood, bullets, shells, and other weapons. Interprets laboratory findings relative to drugs, poisons, narcotics, alcohol, or other compounds ingested or injected into body. Reconstructs crime scene, preserving marks or impressions made by shoes, tires, or other objects by plaster or moulage casts. Prepares reports or presentations of findings, methods, and techniques used to support conclusions, and prepares results for court or other formal hearings. May testify as expert witness on evidence or crime laboratory techniques. Confers with experts in such specialities as ballistics, fingerprinting, handwriting, documents, electronics, metallurgy, biochemistry, medicine, or others.

AMERICAN ACADEMY OF FORENSIC SCIENCES
225 South Academy Boulevard, Suite 201
Colorado Springs, CO 80910

AMERICAN SOCIETY OF CRIME LABORATORY DIRECTORS
c/o Robert W. Horn
New York State Police Laboratory
State Campus Building, 22
Albany, NY 12226

POLICE OFFICER

Patrols assigned beat on foot, using motorcycle or patrol car, or on horseback to control traffic, prevent crime or disturbance of peace, and arrest violators: Familiarizes self with beat and with persons living in area. Notes suspicious persons and establishments and reports to superior officer. Reports hazards. Disperses unruly crowds at public gatherings. Renders first aid at accidents and investigates causes and results of accident. Conducts investigations to locate, arrest, and return fugitives, persons wanted for non-payment of support payments and unemployment insurance compensation fraud, and to locate missing persons: Reviews files and criminal records to develop possible leads, such as previous addresses and aliases. Contacts employers, neighbors, relatives, law enforcement agencies, and other persons to locate person sought. Obtains necessary legal documents, such as warrants or extradition papers, to bring about return of fugitive. Serves warrants and makes arrests to return persons sought. Examines medical and dental X-rays, fingerprints, and other information to identify bodies held in morgue. Completes reports to document information acquired and actions taken. Testifies in court to present evidence regarding cases. Directs and reroutes traffic around fire or other disruption. Inspects public establishments requiring licenses to insure compliance with rules and regulations. Warns or arrests persons violating animal ordinances. Issues tickets to traffic violators. Registers at police call boxes at specified interval or time. Writes and files daily activity report with superior officer. May drive patrol wagon or police ambulance. May notify public works department of location of abandoned vehicles to tow away. May accompany parking meter personnel to protect money collected. May be designated according to assigned duty as AIRPORT SAFETY AND SECURITY OFFICER; TRAFFIC POLICE OFFICER; or according to equipment used as AMBULANCE DRIVER; MOTORCYCLE; MOUNTED POLICE OFFICER. Additional titles: EMERGENCY DETAIL DRIVER; PATROL DRIVER.

AMERICAN FEDERATION OF POLICE
1000 Connecticut Avenue, NW, Suite 9
Washington, DC 20036

INTERNATIONAL BROTHERHOOD OF POLICE OFFICERS
285 Dorchester Avenue
Boston, MA 02127

NATIONAL ASSOCIATION OF POLICE ORGANIZATIONS
Detroit Police Officers Association
6425 Lincoln
Detroit, MI 48202

NATIONAL SHERIFF'S ASSOCIATION
1450 Duke Street
Alexandria, VA 22314

SPECIAL AGENT

Investigates alleged or suspected criminal violations of federal, or state, or local laws to determine if evidence is sufficient to recommend prosecution: Analyzes charge, complaint or allegation of law violation to identify issues involved and types of evidence needed. Assists in determining scope, timing, and direction of investigation. Develops and uses informants to get leads to information. Obtains evidence or establishes facts by interviewing, observing, and interrogating suspects and witnesses and analyzing records. Examines records to detect links in a chain of evidence or information. Uses cameras and photostatic machines to record evidence and documents. Verifies information obtained to establish accuracy and authenticity of facts and evidence. Maintains surveillances and performs undercover assignments. Presents findings in clear, logical, impartial, and properly documented reports. Reports critical information to and coordinates activities with other offices or agencies when applicable. Testifies before grand juries. Serves subpoenas or other official papers. May lead or coordinate work of other SPECIAL AGENTS. May obtain and use search and arrest warrants. May serve on full time, detail, or rotational protection assignments. May carry firearms and make arrests. May be designated according to agency worked for, as SPECIAL AGENT, FBI; SPECIAL AGENT, SECRET SERVICE.

FEDERAL BUREAU OF INVESTIGATION
U.S. Department of Justice
Washington, DC 20535

OFFICE OF PUBLIC AFFAIRS
U.S. Secret Service
Department of the Treasury
1800 G Street, NW
Washington, DC 20223

LOBBYING

*Warning! Stay within the **industries** of this book. For example, education lobbyist.*

LOBBYIST

Contacts and confers with members of legislature and other holders of public office to persuade them to support legislation favorable to client's interests: Studies proposed legislation to determine possible effect on interest of client, who may be a person, specific group, or general public. Confers with legislators and officials to emphasize supposed weaknesses or merits of specific bills to influence passage, defeat, or amendment of measure or introduction of legislation more favorable to client's interests. Contacts individuals and groups having similar interests in order to encourage them also to contact legislators and present views. Prepares news releases and informational pamphlets and conducts news conferences in order to state client's views and to inform public of features of proposed legislation considered desirable or undesirable. May contact regulatory agencies and testify at public hearings to enlist support for client's interests. May be legally required to register with governmental authorities as lobbyist and to submit reports of regulated expenditures incurred during lobbying activities.

AMERICAN LEAGUE OF LOBBYISTS
P.O. Box 20450
Alexandria, VA 22320

LOCKSMITHING

LOCKSMITH
Repairs and opens locks, makes keys, changes lock combinations, using handtools and special equipment: Disassembles locks, such as padlocks, safe locks, and door locks, and repairs or replaces worn tumblers, springs, and other parts. Shortens tumblers, using file, and inserts new or repaired tumblers into lock to change combination. Cuts new or duplicate keys, using keycutting machine. Moves lockpick in cylinder to open door locks without keys. Opens safe locks by listening to lock sounds or by drilling. May keep records of company locks and keys. Recommends security measures to customers. May install electronic burglar alarms and surveillance systems.

ASSOCIATED LOCKSMITHS OF AMERICA
3003 Live Oak Street
Dallas, TX 75204

LOCKSMITH SECURITY ASSOCIATION
32630 Concord Drive
Madison Heights, MI 48071

MEDICAL

ACUPRESSURIST
Examines patients and analyzes findings to diagnose and treat physical problems

according to knowledge and techniques of acupressure: Directs patient to lie on treatment couch and positions patient's arms and legs in relaxed position to facilitate examination and treatment. Examines patient's muscular system visually and feels tissue around muscles, nerves, and blood vessels to locate knots and other blockages which indicate excessive accumulations of blood, water, and other substances in tissue. Determines cause of accumulations and treatment procedures, according to knowledge of acupressure and experience. Discusses findings with patient and explains relationship to internal organs. Outlines course of treatment for patient and advises patient regarding methods and diet for prevention of problem recurrence. Uses specific method or combination of acupressure methods, such as Ghi Ahp, Jin Shin Do, or Shiatsu, and may be known accordingly.

AMERICAN ASSOCIATION FOR ACUPUNCTURE & ORIENTAL MEDICINE
5473 66th Street North
St. Petersburg, FL 33709

ACUPUNCTURIST
Administers specific therapeutic treatment of symptoms and disorders amenable to acupuncture procedures, as specifically indicated by supervising Physician: Reviews patient's medical history, physical findings, and diagnosis made by PHYSICIAN to ascertain symptoms or disorder to be treated. Selects needles of various lengths, according to location of insertion. Inserts needles at locations of body known to be efficacious to certain disorders, utilizing knowledge of acupuncture points and their functions. Leaves needles in patient for specific length of time, according to symptom or disorder treated, and removes needles. Burns bark of mugwort tree in small strainer to administer moxibustion treatment. Covers insertion area with cloth to impart heat and assist in relieving patient's symptoms.

AMERICAN ACUPUNCTURE ASSOCIATION
4262 Kissena Boulevard
Flushing, NY 11355

AMERICAN ASSOCIATION FOR ACUPUNCTURE & ORIENTAL MEDICINE
5473 66th Street North
St. Petersburg, FL 33709

ALLERGIST-IMMUNOLOGIST
Diagnoses and treats diseases and conditions with allergic or immunologic causes: Examines patient, utilizing diagnostic aids, such as X-ray machine, stethoscope, thermometer, patch tests, and blood tests. Elicits and records information about patient's history. Analyzes reports and test results and prescribes treatment or

medication for conditions, such as bronchial asthma, dermatalogical disorders, connective tissue syndromes, transplantation, and auto-immunity. Refers patients to available ancillary and consultant services when necessary for patient's well-being.

AMERICAN ACADEMY OF ALLERGY & IMMUNOLOGY
611 East Wells Street
Milwaukee, WI 53202

AMERICAN COLLEGE OF ALLERGY & IMMUNOLOGY
800 East Northwest Highway, Suite 1080
Palantine, IL 60067

ANESTHESIOLOGIST

Administers anesthetics to render patients insensible to pain during surgical, obstetrical, and other medical procedures: Examines patient to determine degree of surgical risk, and type of anesthesia and sedation to administer, and discuss findings with medical practitioner concerned with case. Positions patient on operating table and administers local, intravenous, spinal, caudal, or other anesthetic according to prescribed medical standards. Institutes remedial measures to counteract adverse reactions or complications. Records type and amount of anesthetic and sedation administered and condition of patient before, during, and after anesthesia. May instruct medical students and other personnel in characteristics and methods of administering various types of anesthetics, signs and symptoms of reactions and complications, and emergency measures to employ.

AMERICAN SOCIETY OF ANESTHESIOLOGISTS
515 Vusse Highway
Park Ridge, IL 60068

AMERICAN SOCIETY OF REGIONAL ANESTHESIA
P.O. Box 11086
Richmond, VA 23230

INTERNATIONAL ANESTHESIA RESEARCH SOCIETY
3645 Warrensville Center Road
Cleveland, OH 44122

AUDIOLOGIST

Specializes in evaluation of hearing, prevention, habilitative and rehabilitative services for auditory problems, and research related to hearing and attendant disorders: Determines range, nature and degree of hearing function related to patient's auditory efficiency (communication needs), using electroacoustic instrumentation, such as pure-tone and speech audiometers, and acoustic impedance equipment. Coordinates audiometric results with other diagnostic data, such as educational, medical, social, and behavioral information. Differentiates between organic and nonorganic hearing disabilities through evaluation of total response pattern and use of acoustic tests, such as Stenger and electrodermal audiometry. Plans, directs, conducts, or participates in conservation, habilitative and rehabilitative programs including hearing aid selection and orientation, counseling, guidance, auditory training, speech reading, language habilitation, and speech conservation. May conduct research in physiology, pathology, biophysics, and psychophysics of auditory systems. May design and develop clinical and research procedures and apparatus. May act as consultant to educational, medical, and other professional groups. May teach art and science of audiology and direct scientific projects. May specialize in fields, such as industrial audiology, geriatric audiology, pediatric audiology, and research audiology. See SPEECH PATHOLOGIST for one who specializes in diagnosis and treatment of speech and language problems.

ACADEMY OF DISPENSING AUDIOLOGISTS
900 Des Moines, Suite 200
Des Moines, IA 50309

AMERICAN AUDITORY SOCIETY
1966 Inwood Road
Dallas, TX 75235

CARDIOLOGIST

Treats diseases of heart and its functions: Examines patient for symptoms indicative of heart disorders, using stethoscope, electrocardiograph, X-ray machine, and variety of laboratory equipment. Studies X-ray photographs and electrocardiograph recordings to aid in making diagnoses. Prescribes medications, and recommends dietary and work activity program, as indicated. Refers patient to SURGEON specializing in cardiac cases when need for corrective surgery is indicated. May engage in research to study anatomy of and diseases peculiar to heart.

AMERICAN COLLEGE OF CARDIOLOGY
9111 Old Georgetown Road
Bethesda, MD 20814

AMERICAN SOCIETY OF ECHOCARDIOGRAPHY
1100 Raleigh Building
Five West Hargett Street
Raleigh, NC 27601

CARDIOPULMONARY TECHNOLOGIST

Performs diagnostic tests of cardiovascular and pulmonary systems of patients in hospital, using variety of laboratory machines and other work devices, to aid physicians in diagnosis and treatment: Conducts electrocardiogram, phonocardiography, vectorcardiography, ultrasound, stress, cardiac catherization, blood pressure, and other vascular tests to diagnose disorders of cardiovascular system, using variety of laboratory equipment, such as electrocardiograph and phonocardiograph machines, stethoscope, and catheter. Conducts tests of pulmonary system to diagnose pulmonary disorders, using respiratory equipment. Analyzes and interprets test findings and furnishes results to physician.

AMERICAN CARDIOLOGY TECHNOLOGISTS ASSOCIATION
1980 Isaac Newton Square South
Reston, VA 22090

ASSOCIATION OF PHYSICIANS ASSISTANTS IN CARDIOVASCULAR SURGERY
217 Hillcrest Street
Orlando, FL 32801

NATIONAL SOCIETY FOR CARDIOVASCULAR & PULMONARY TECHNOLOGY
1133 15th Street, NW, Suite 1000
Washington, DC 20005

AMERICAN MEDICAL TECHNOLOGISTS
710 Higgins Road
Park Ridge, IL 60068

CENTRAL SUPPLY WORKER, MEDICAL

Cleans, sterilizes, and assembles hospital equipment, supplies, and instruments according to prescribed procedures and techniques performing any combination of following tasks: Scrubs and washes surgical instruments, containers, and syringes and equipment, such as aspirators, croupettes, and oxygen suppliers. Sterilizes instruments, equipment, surgical linens, and supplies, such as surgical packs, treatment trays, and syringes, using autoclave, water sterilizer, or antiseptic solutions. Prepares packs of supplies and instruments, and dressing and treatment trays, according to designated lists or codes, and wraps, labels, and seals packs. Sharpens hypodermic needles, using hone or abrasive wheel, and matches syringe barrels and plungers, according to size, trade names, or serial number. Stores prepared articles and supplies in designated areas. May fill requisitions, write charges, and inventory supplies. May prepare solutions according to prescribed formula. May be assigned to such hospital rooms as surgery and delivery rooms. May be required to hold Practical Nurse license.

AMERICAN MEDICAL TECHNOLOGISTS
710 Higgins Road
Park Ridge, IL 60068

CHEMISTRY TECHNOLOGIST

Performs qualitative and quantitative chemical analyses of body fluids and exudates, following manual instructions, to provide information used in diagnosing and treating diseases: Tests body specimens, such as urine, blood, spinal fluid, and gastric juices, for presence and quantity of metabolic substances and byproducts, such as sugar, albumin, and acetone bodies; and for various chemicals, drugs, and poisons. Prepares solutions used in chemical analysis. Calibrates and maintains spectrophotometers, colorimeters, flame photometers, and other equipment used in quantitative and qualitative analysis.

AMERICAN MEDICAL TECHNOLOGISTS
710 Higgins Road
Park Ridge, IL 60068

CHIROPRACTOR

Adjusts spinal column and other articulations of body to prevent disease and correct abnormalities of human body believed to be caused by interference with nervous system: Examines patient to determine nature and extent of disorder, using X-ray machine, electrocardiograph, otoscope, proctoscope, and other instruments and equipment. Manipulates spine or other involved area. May utilize supplementary measures, such as exercise, rest, water, light, heat, and nutritional therapy.

AMERICAN CHIROPRACTIC ASSOCIATION
1701 Clarendon Boulevard
Arlington, VA 22209

ASSOCIATION OF CHIROPRACTIC COLLEGES
6401 Rockhill Road
Kansas City, MO 64131

PARKER CHIROPRACTIC RESEARCH FOUNDATION
P.O. Box 40444
Ft. Worth, TX 76140

CYTOTECHNOLOGIST

Stains, mounts, and studies cells of human body to determine pathological condition: Examines specimen, and diagnoses nature and extent of disease or cellular damage. Executes variety of laboratory tests and analyses to confirm findings. Reports information to PATHOLOGIST.

AMERICAN SOCIETY FOR CYTOLOGY
1015 Chestnut Street, Suite 1518
Philadelphia, PA 19107

AMERICAN SOCIETY FOR CYTOTECHNOLOGY
10480 Gregory Circle
Cypress, CA 90630

DERMATOLOGIST

Diagnoses and treats diseases of human skin: Examines skin to determine nature of disease, taking blood samples, smears from affected areas, and performing other laboratory procedures. Examines specimens under microscope, and makes various chemical and biological analyses and performs other tests to identify disease-causing organisms or pathological conditions. Prescribes and administers medications, and applies superficial radiotherapy and other localized treatments. Treats abscesses, accidental skin injuries, and other skin infections, and surgically excises cutaneous malignancies, cysts, birthmarks, and other growths. Treats scars, using dermabrasion.

AMERICAN ACADEMY OF DERMATOLOGY
1567 Maple Avenue
Evanston, IL 60201

NATIONAL PSORIASIS FOUNDATION
6443 Southwest Beaverton Highway, Suite 210
Portland, OR 97221

DIALYSIS TECHNICIAN

Sets up and operates artificial kidney machine to provide dialyses treatment for patients with kidney disorders or failure: Attaches coil, tubing, and connectors to machine to assemble it for use. Mixes priming, heparin, dialysis, and other solutions, according to formula. Primes coil with saline solution, heparinized solution, and whole blood to prepare machine for osmotic action. Transports patient to dialysis room and positions patient on cart at kidney machine. Takes and records patient's predialysis weight, temperature, blood pressure, pulse rate, and respiration rate. Removes shunt dressing from patient's arm or leg and takes blood sample from artery shunt. Connects kidney machine coil tubes to artery shunt and vein shunt in patient's arm or leg to start blood circulating through coil. Takes osmolality reading of dialysis bath solution to insure solution is at specified strength, and fills circulating tank of kidney machine with solution. Starts electric pump that circulates solution through and around kidney coil to activate osmosis between blood in coil and dialysis solution in circulating tank to remove impurities from blood. Monitors patient for adverse reaction and kidney machine for malfunction. Adjusts machine to maintain temperature of solution in coil at compatible level with blood in patient's circulatory system. Takes periodic blood pressure readings and performs hematocrit and clotting time tests on patient's blood sample during dialysis. Administers oxygen or gives blood transfusion as required. Takes blood samples and removes tubes from shunts at end of treatment. Takes reading of vital signs and records readings on chart. Inspects shunts for leakage and bandages shunts. Drains blood from coil and returns it to blood bank for reuse by patient, and delivers blood sample to laboratory for analysis. Cleans and sterilizes kidney machine and reusable connectors. Packs permanent tubing and connectors in sterile containers. Makes parts, such as connectors and shunts, from materials such as plastic tubing and coated plastic. May assist with surgical insertion of shunts into vein and artery of patient's arm or leg. May explain dialysis procedure and operation of kidney machine to patient before first treatment to allay apprehension or fear of dialysis. May operate dialysis machine equipped with membrane instead of coil.

AMERICAN MEDICAL TECHNOLOGISTS
710 Higgins Road
Park Ridge, IL 60068

INTERNATIONAL SOCIETY OF PERITONEAL DIALYSIS
Nephrology Division
Georgetown University Hospital
Washington, DC 20007

NATIONAL KIDNEY FOUNDATION
Two Park Avenue
New York, NY 10003

DOCTOR, NATUROPATHIC

Diagnoses, treats, and cares for patients, using system of practice that bases treatment of physiological functions and abnormal conditions on natural laws governing human body: Utilizes physiological, psychological, and mechanical methods, such as air, water, light, heat, earth, phytotherapy, food and herb therapy, psychotherapy, electrotherapy, physiotherapy, minor and orificial surgery, mechanotherapy, naturopathic corrections and manipulation, and natural methods or modalities, together with natural medicines, natural processed foods, and herbs and nature's remedies. Excludes major surgery, therapeutic use of X-ray and radium, and use of drugs, except those assimilable substances containing elements or compounds which are components of body tissues and are physiologically compatible to body processes for maintenance of life.

AMERICAN HOLISTIC MEDICAL ASSOCIATION
2002 Eastlake Avenue East
Seattle, WA 98102

INTERNATIONAL ASSOCIATION OF HOLISTIC HEALTH PRACTITIONERS
3419 Thom Boulevard
Las Vegas, NV 89130

ELECTROCARDIOGRAPH TECHNICIAN

Records electromotive variations in action of heart muscle, using electrocardio-graph machine, to provide data for diagnosis of heart ailments: Attaches electrodes to specified areas of patient's body. Turns selector switch, and moves chest electrode to successive positions across chest to record electromotive variations occurring in various areas of heart muscle. Presses button to mark tracing paper to indicate positions of chest electrodes. Replenishes supply of paper and ink in machine and reports malfunctions. Edits and mounts final results and forwards results to CARDIOLOGIST for analysis and interpretation.

AMERICAN MEDICAL TECHNOLOGISTS
710 Higgins Road
Park Ridge, IL 60068

ELECTROENCEPHALOGRAPHIC TECHNOLOGIST

Measures impulse frequencies and differences in electrical potential from brain for use in diagnosis of brain disorders, using electroencephalograph: Fastens electrode to patient's head, using adhesive tape, adhesive paste, or pins inserted into skull epidermis according to specified pattern. Attaches electrode terminals to switchbox and turns selector switches to obtain combinations for complete set of graphic readings. Observes patient's behavior and makes notes on graph. Makes minor adjustments and repairs to equipment, such as replacing condensers and refilling tracing pins. Monitors other variables, such as electromyograms, electrocardiograms, electrooculograms, and respiration as directed.

AMERICAN ELECTROENCEPHALOGRAPHIC SOCIETY
2579 Melinda Drive
Atlanta, GA 30345

AMERICAN MEDICAL TECHNOLOGISTS
710 Higgins Road
Park Ridge, IL 60068

AMERICAN SOCIETY OF ELECTRONEURODIAGNOSTIC TECHNOLOGISTS
Sixth at Quint
Carrol, IA 51401

FAMILY PRACTITIONER

Provides comprehensive medical services for members of family, regardless of age or sex, on continuing basis: Examines patients, utilizing diagnostic aids, such as stethoscope, sphygmomanometer, thermometer, and other instruments. Elicits and records information about patient's medical history. Orders or executes various tests, analyses, and X-rays to provide information on patient's condition. Analyzes reports and findings of tests and examination, and diagnoses condition. Administers or prescribes treatments and medications. Promotes health by advising patients concerning diet, hygiene, and methods for prevention of disease. Inoculates and vaccinates patients to immunize them from communicable diseases. Provides prenatal care to pregnant women, delivers babies, and provides postnatal care to mothers and infants (OBSTETRICIAN). Performs surgical procedures commensurate with surgical competency. Refers patients to medical specialist for consultant services when necessary for patient's well-being.

AMERICAN ACADEMY OF FAMILY PHYSICIANS
8880 Ward Parkway
Kansas City, MO 64114

GENERAL PRACTITIONER

Attends to variety of medical cases in general practice: Examines patients, utilizing stethoscope, sphygmomanometer, and other instruments. Orders or executes various tests, analyses, and X-rays to provide information on patient's condition. Analyzes reports and findings of tests and of examination, and diagnoses condition. Administers or prescribes treatments and drugs. Inoculates and vaccinates patients to immunize them from communicable diseases. Promotes health by advising patients concerning diet, hygiene, and methods for prevention of disease. Provides prenatal care to pregnant women, delivers babies, and provides postnatal care to mother and infant (OBSTETRICIAN). Reports births, deaths, and outbreak of contagious diseases to governmental authorities. May make house and emergency calls to attend to patients unable to visit office or clinic. May conduct physical examinations of insurance company applicants to determine health and risk involved in insuring applicant. May provide care for passengers and crew aboard ship and be designated SURGEON.

AMERICAN ACADEMY OF FAMILY PHYSICIANS
8880 Ward Parkway
Kansas City, MO 64114

GYNECOLOGIST

Diagnoses and treats diseases and disorders of female genital, urinary, and rectal organs: Examines patient to determine medical problem, utilizing physical and radiological examination findings, laboratory test results, and patient's statements as diagnostic aids. Discusses problem with patient, and prescribes medication, appropriate exercise or hygiene regimes, or performs surgery as needed to correct malfunctions or remove diseased organ. May care for patient throughout pregnancy and deliver babies (OBSTETRICIAN).

AMERICAN COLLEGE OF OBSTETRICIANS & GYNECOLOGISTS
600 Maryland Avenue, SW, Suite 300 E
Washington, DC 20024

HOLTER SCANNING TECHNICIAN

Analyzes tape from cardiac-function monitoring device worn by patient to provide data for diagnosis of cardiovascular disorders: Places magnetic tape from heart monitor worn by patient during specified test period into spindle of tape scanner and pushes button to activate scanner. Turns knobs on scanner to adjust controls that regulate taped sounds associated with heart activity and focus video representation of sounds on screen of scanner. Observes scanner screen to identify irregularities in patient cardiac patterns, utilizing knowledge of regular and irregular cardiac-function patterns. Presses button on scanner to activate printer that prints sections of tape showing abnormal cardiac patterns. Tears strip of tape from printer and measures distances between peaks and valleys of heart activity patterns, using calipers, to obtain data for further analysis. Records findings on laboratory report forms and forwards tapes and forms to designated personnel. May fit patient with heart monitor, following instructions of supervisory personnel. May analyze patient diary to identify incidents that correspond to heart pattern irregularities detected on monitor tape. May perform other diagnostic procedures, such as electrocardiography and stress testing, to aid in medical evaluation of patient.

AMERICAN MEDICAL TECHNOLOGISTS
710 Higgins Road
Park Ridge, IL 60068

HOME HEALTH TECHNICIAN

Provides patient care, assistance, and instructions in household management and in-home medical care techniques to patients and families in home or homelike environment: Assists ambulatory and bedridden patient with dressing, bathing, grooming, and elimination. Transfers patient to and from wheelchair, and helps patient to walk to and from bed, shower, tub, and lavatory. Performs procedures and treatments as directed by professional staff, such as massages, hot and cold applications, dressing changes, wound irrigation, enemas, douches, catheterizations, and ostomy care, utilizing knowledge of body structures and function and aseptic techniques. Administers oral medications and injections under medical supervision. Measures and records patient temperature, pulse, and respiration rates, blood pressure, fluid intake and output, and performs throat inspection and urine tests to provide data for health-care team assessment. Teaches patients and family members approved medical techniques, such as mobility training in use of walkers, crutches, and other range-of-motion and supportive devices, to enable continuing home care, utilizing knowledge of physical rehabilitation techniques. Demonstrates basic home management techniques, such as housekeeping, nutrition, meal planning and preparation, and adapts techniques to patient's physical limitations. Guides and encourages patient and family to obtain optimal adjustment to illness or disability.

AMERICAN FEDERATION OF HOME HEALTH AGENCIES
1320 Fenwick Lane, Suite 500
Silver Spring, MD 20910

AMERICAN MEDICAL TECHNOLOGISTS
710 Higgins Road
Park Ridge, IL 60068

NATIONAL ASSOCIATION FOR HOME CARE
519 C Street, NE
Stanton Park
Washington, DC 20002

IMMUNOHEMATOLOGIST

Performs immunohematology tests, recommends blood problem solutions to doctors, and serves blood bank and community as consultant and instructor: Visually analyzes blood in specimen tubes to determine temperature and speed of centrifuge for starting hematology tests. Centrifuges blood specimen to separate red cells from serum and examines separated cells to detect presence of antibodies. Interprets evidence observed to devise experiments and suggest techniques that will resolve patient's blood problems. Combines known and unknown serums with red cells in test tubes and selects reagents, such as albumin, protolytic enzymes, and antihuman globulin, for individual tests to enhance and make visible reactions of agglutination and hemolysis. Precesses various combinations in centrifuge and examines resulting samples under microscope to identify evidence of agglutination or hemolysis. Repeats and varies tests until normal suspension of reagents, serum, and red cells is attained. Writes blood specifications to meet patient's need, on basis of test results, and applies knowledge of blood classification system to locate donor's blood. Performs hematology tests on donor's blood to confirm matching blood types. Requisitions and sends blood to supply patient's need, and prepares written report to inform physician of test results and of required volume of blood to administer. Forwards copy of report to furnish data input for computer files. Studies worksheets to evaluate completeness of hematology tests and reads labels of related specimen tubes to identify known patients. Instructs MEDICAL LABORATORY TECHNICIANS in classroom, in work situations, and over telephone to teach techniques of microscopic identification of precipitation, agglutination, or hemolysis in blood that leads to resolutions of problems. Writes notes on worksheets of MEDICAL LABORATORY TECHNICIANS to suggest possible solutions for specific problems and returns worksheets and specimens to aid personnel in blood bank reference library.

AMERICAN SOCIETY OF HEMATOLOGY
c/o Ira Weiss
Slack, Inc.
6900 Grove Road
Thorofare, NJ 08086

INTERNIST

Diagnoses and treats diseases and injuries of human internal organ systems: Examines patient for symptoms of organic or congenital disorders and determines nature and extent of injury or disorder, using diagnostic aids, such as X-ray machine, blood tests, electrocardiograph, sphgmomanometer, and stethoscope. Prescribes medication and recommends dietary and activity program, as indicated by diagnosis. Refers patient to appropriate medical specialist when indicated.

AMERICAN BOARD OF INTERNAL MEDICINE
3624 Market Street
Philadelphia, PA 19104

MEDICAL ASSISTANT

Performs following duties under direction of Physician in examination and treatment of patients: Prepares treatment rooms for examination of patient. Drapes patients with covering and positions instruments and equipment. Hands instruments and materials to doctor as directed. Sterilizes and cleans instruments. Prepares inventory of supplies to determine items to be replenished. Interviews patients and checks pulse, temperature, blood pressure, weight, and height. May operate equipment, give injections or treatments, and assist in laboratory. May schedule appointments, receive money for bills, keep X-ray and other medical records, perform secretarial tasks, complete insurance forms, and maintain financial records.

AMERICAN ASSOCIATION OF MEDICAL ASSISTANTS
20 North Wacker Drive, Suite 1575
Chicago, IL 60606

MEDICAL PHYSICIST

Applies knowledge and methodology of science of physics to all aspects of medicine, to address problems related to diagnosis and treatment of human disease: Advises and consults with PHYSICIANS in such applications as use of ionizing radiation in diagnosis, therapy, treatment planning with externally delivered radiation as well as use of internally implanted radioactive sources; complete subject of X-ray equipment, calibration, and dosimetry; medical uses of ultrasound and infrared; bioelectrical investigation of brain and heart; mathematical analysis and applications of computers in medicine; formulation of radiation protection guides and procedures specific to hospital environment; development of instrumentation for improved patient care and clinical service. Plans, directs, conducts, and participates in supporting programs to insure effective and safe use of radiation and radionuclides in human beings by PHYSICIAN specialist. Teaches principles of medical physics to PHYSICIANS, residents, graduate students, medical students, and technologists by means of lectures, problem solving, and laboratory sessions. Directs and participates in investigations of biophysical techniques associated with any branch of medicine. Conducts research in development of diagnostic and remedial procedures and develops instrumentation for specific medical applications. Acts as consultant to education, medical research, and other professional groups and organizations.

AMERICAN ASSOCIATION OF PHYSICISTS IN MEDICINE
335 East 45th Street
New York, NY 10017

MEDICAL-RECORDS ADMINISTRATOR

Plans, develops, and administers medical record systems for hospital, clinic, health center, or similar facility, to meet standards of accrediting and regulatory agencies: Collects and analyzes patient and institutional data. Assists medical staff in evaluating quality of patient care and in developing criteria and methods for such evaluation. Develops and implements policies and procedures for documenting, storing, retrieving information, and for processing medical-legal documents, insurance and correspondence requests, in conformance with federal, state, and local statutes. Develops in-service educational materials and conducts instructional programs for health care personnel. Supervises staff in preparing and analyzing medical documents. Provides consultant services to health care facilities, health data systems, related health organizations, and governmental agencies. Engages in basic and applied research in health care field.

AMERICAN MEDICAL RECORDS ASSOCIATION
John Hancock Center, Suite 1850
875 North Michigan Avenue
Chicago, IL 60611

MEDICAL TECHNOLOGISTS

Medical technologists perform complicated chemical, biological, hematological, immunologic, microscopic, and bacteriological tests. These may include chemical tests to determine blood cholesterol levels or microscopic examinations of blood and other substances to detect the presence of diseases such as leukemia. They receive specimens, or obtain such body materials as urine, blood, pus, and tissue directly from the patient. Technologists microscopically examine body constituents; make cultures of body fluid or tissue samples to determine the presence of bacteria, fungi, parasites, or other micro-organisms; and analyze samples for chemical content or reaction. They cut stain and mount tissue sections for study by a PATHOLOGIST. They also type and cross-match blood samples for transfusions. Most medical technologists perform tests ordered by PHYSICIANS for their patients. Others conduct research, develop laboratory techniques, teach, or assume laboratory management and administrative duties. Some technologists work as independent consultants, advising physicians on how to set up and operate office laboratories. Others work in product development and sales.

AMERICAN MEDICAL TECHNOLOGISTS
710 Higgins Road
Park Ridge, IL 60068

INTERNATIONAL SOCIETY FOR CLINICAL LABORATORY TECHNOLOGY
818 Olive Street, Suite 918
St. Louis, MO 63101

NATIONAL CERTIFICATION FOR MEDICAL LABORATORY PERSONNEL
1725 De Sales Street, NW, Suite 403
Washington, DC 20036

NATIONAL COMMITTEE FOR CLINICAL LABORATORY STANDARDS
771 East Lancaster Avenue
Villanova, PA 19085

MICROBIOLOGY TECHNOLOGIST

Cultivate, isolates, and assists in identifying bacteria and other micro-organisms, and performs various bacteriological, mycological, virological, and parasitological tests: Receives human or animal body materials from autopsy or diagnostic cases, or collects specimens directly from patients, under supervision of laboratory director. Examines material for evidence of disease of parasites. Makes parasitological tests of specimens concentrated or inoculated on culture media.

AMERICAN MEDICAL TECHNOLOGISTS
710 Higgins Road
Park Ridge, IL 60068

AMERICAN ACADEMY OF MICROBIOLOGY
1913 Eye Street
Washington, DC 20006

INTERNATIONAL SOCIETY FOR CLINICAL LABORATORY TECHNOLOGY
818 Olive Street, Suite 918
St. Louis, MO 63101

NATIONAL CERTIFICATION FOR MEDICAL LABORATORY PERSONNEL
1725 De Sales Street, NW, Suite 403
Washington, DC 20036

NATIONAL COMMITTEE FOR CLINICAL LABORATORY STANDARDS
771 East Lancaster Avenue
Villanova, PA 19085

NEUROLOGIST

Diagnoses and treats organic diseases and disorders of nervous system: Orders and studies results of chemical, microscopic, biological, and bacteriological analyses of patient's blood and cerebro-spinal fluid to determine nature and extent of disease or disorder. Identifies presence of pathological blood conditions or parasites and prescribes and administers medications and drugs. Orders and studies results of electroencephalograms or X-rays to detect abnormalities in brain wave patterns, or indications of abnormalities in brain structure. Advises patient to contact NEUROSURGEON when need for surgery is indicated.

AMERICAN ACADEMY OF NEUROLOGY
2221 University Avenue, SE, Suite 335
Minneapolis, MN 55414

NUCLEAR MEDICAL TECHNOLOGIST

Prepares, administers, and measures radioactive isotopes in therapeutic, diagnostic, and tracer studies, utilizing variety of radioisotope equipment: Prepares stock solutions of radioactive materials, and calculates doses to be administered by RADIOLOGIST. Measures glandular activity, traces radioactive doses, and calculates amount of radiation, using equipment, such as Geiger counters, electroscopes, scalers, scintillation and position scanners, and scintigrams. Calibrates equipment. Subjects patients to radiation as prescribed by RADIOLO-GIST, using such equipment as radium emanation tubes and needles, X-ray machines, and similar instruments. Executes blood volume, red cell survival, and fat absorption studies, following standard laboratory techniques.

AMERICAN MEDICAL TECHNOLOGISTS
710 Higgins Road
Park Ridge, IL 60068

TECHNOLOGIST SECTION OF THE SOCIETY OF NUCLEAR MEDICINE
136 Madison Avenue
New York, NY 10016

NURSE ANESTHETIST

Administers intravenous, spinal, and other anesthetics to render persons insensible to pain during surgical operations, deliveries, or other medical and dental procedures: Positions patient and administers prescribed anesthetic in accordance with standardized procedures, regulating flow of gases or injecting fluids intravenously or rectally. Observes patient's reaction during anesthesia, periodically counting pulse and respiration, taking blood pressure, and noting skin color and dilatation of pupils. Administers oxygen or initiates other emergency measures to prevent surgical shock, asphyxiation, or other adverse conditions. Informs PHYSICIAN of patient's condition during anesthesia. Records patient's preoperative, operative, and postoperative condition, anesthetic and medications administered, and related data. May give patient postoperative care as directed.

AMERICAN NURSE'S ASSOCIATION
2420 Pershing Road
Kansas City, MO 64108

COUNCIL ON CERTIFICATION OF NURSE ANESTHETIST
216 Higgins Road
Park Ridge, IL 600068

NURSE, CONSULTANT

Advises hospitals, schools of nursing, industrial organizations, and public health groups on problems related to nursing activities and health services: Reviews and suggests changes in nursing organization and administrative procedures. Analyzes nursing techniques and recommends modifications. Aids schools in planning nursing curriculums, and hospitals and public health nursing services in developing and carrying out staff education programs. Provides assistance in developing guides and manuals for specific aspects of nursing services. Prepares educational materials and assists in planning and developing health and educational programs for industrial and community groups. Advises in services available through community resources. Consults with nursing groups concerning professional and educational problems. Prepares or furnishes data for articles and lectures. Participates in surveys and research studies.

AMERICAN NURSE'S ASSOCIATION
2420 Pershing Road
Kansas City, MO 64108

NURSE CONSULTANTS ASSOCIATION
P.O. Box 25875
Colorado Springs, CO 80936

NURSE, INSTRUCTOR

Demonstrates and teaches patient care in classroom and clinical units to nursing students and instructs students in principles and application of physical, biological, and psychological subjects related to nursing: Lectures to students, conducts and supervises laboratory work, issues assignments, and directs seminars and panels. Prepares and administers examinations, evaluates student progress, and maintains records of student classroom and clinical experience. Participates in planning curriculum, teaching schedule, and course outline. Cooperates with medical and nursing personnel in evaluating and improving teaching and nursing practices. May specialize in specific subject, such as anatomy, chemistry, psychology, or nutrition, or in type of nursing activity, such as nursing of medical or surgical patients.

AMERICAN NURSE'S ASSOCIATION
2420 Pershing Road
Kansas City, MO 64108

NURSE, LICENSED PRACTICAL

Cares for ill, injured, convalescent, and handicapped persons in hospitals, clinics, private homes, sanitariums, and similar institutions: Takes and records temperature, blood pressure, and pulse and respiration rate. Dresses wounds, gives enemas, douches, alcohol rubs, and massages. Applies compresses, ice bags, and hot water bottles. Observes patient and reports adverse reactions to medical personnel in charge. Administers specified medication, and notes time and amount on patient's chart. Assembles and uses such equipment as catheters, tracheotomy tubes, and oxygen suppliers. Performs routine laboratory work, such as urinalysis. Sterilizes equipment and supplies, using germicides, sterilizer, or autoclave. Prepares food trays and feeds patient. Records food and fluid intake and output. Bathes, dresses, and assists patient in walking and turning. Cleans rooms, makes beds, and answers patient's calls. Washes and dresses bodies of deceased persons. Must pass state board examination and be licensed. May assist in delivery, care, and feeding of infants.

AMERICAN NURSE'S ASSOCIATION
2420 Pershing Road
Kansas City, MO 64108

NURSE, PRIVATE DUTY

Contracts independently to render nursing care, usually to one patient, in hospital or private home: Administers medications, treatments, dressings, and other nursing services, according to PHYSICIAN'S instructions and condition of patient. Observes, evaluates, and records symptoms. Applies independent emergency measures to counteract adverse developments and notifies PHYSICIAN of patient's condition. Directs patient in good health habits. Gives information to family in treatment of patient and maintenance of healthful environment. Maintains equipment and supplies. Cooperates with community agencies furnishing assistance to patient. May supervise diet when employed in private home. May specialize in one field of nursing, such as obstetrics, psychiatry, or tuberculosis.

AMERICAN NURSE'S ASSOCIATION
2420 Pershing Road
Kansas City, MO 64108

OBSTETRICIAN

Treats women during prenatal, natal, and postnatal periods: Examines patient to ascertain condition, utilizing physical findings, laboratory results, and patient's statements as diagnostic aids. Determines need for modified diet and physical activities, and recommends plan. Periodically examines patient, prescribing medication or surgery, if indicated. Delivers infant, and cares for mother for prescribed period of time following childbirth. Performs cesarean section or other surgical procedure as needed to preserve patient's health and deliver infant safely. May treat patients for diseases of generative organs (GYNECOLOGIST).

AMERICAN COLLEGE OF OBSTETRICIANS & GYNECOLOGISTS
600 Maryland Avenue, SW, Suite 300 E
Washington, DC 20024

OPHTHALMOLOGIST

Diagnoses and treats diseases and injuries of eyes: Examines patient for symptoms indicative of organic or congenital ocular disorders, and determines nature and extent of injury or disorder. Performs various tests to determine vision loss. Prescribes and administers medications, and performs surgery, if indicated. Directs remedial activities to aid in regaining vision, or to utilize sight remaining, by writing prescriptions for corrective glasses, and instructing patient in eye exercises.

AMERICAN ACADEMY OF OPHTHALMOLOGY
P.O. Box 7424
San Francisco, CA 94120

OPTICIAN

Sets up and operates machine tools to fabricate optical elements and systems, applying knowledge of layout and machining techniques and procedures, shop mathematics, and properties of optical and abrasive materials: Studies work order, blueprints, and sketches to formulate machining plans and sequences. Measures and marks dimensions and reference points to lay out stock for machining. Selects premixed compounds or mixes grinding, polishing, and holding compounds according to formula. Mounts workpiece on holding fixture, using adhesive, friction, or vacuum. Mounts and secures workpiece and tooling in machines. Operates machines, such as saws, lathes, grinders, milling machines, generators, polishers, and edgers to fabricate optics, fixtures, tools, and mountings of specified sizes and shapes. Grinds and polishes optics, using handtools, as required. Measures and tests optics, using precision measuring and testing instruments. May develop specifications and drawings from verbal description. May perform experimental work and research to develop new production methods and procedures applying shop mathematics and knowledge of production techniques. May train and direct other workers.

CONTACT LENS SOCIETY OF AMERICA
P.O. Box 10115
Fairfax, VA 22030

GUILD OF PRESCRIPTION OPTICIANS OF AMERICA
Opticians Associations of America
10341 Democracy Lane
P.O. Box 10110
Fairfax, VA 22030

NATIONAL ASSOCIATION OF MANUAL OPTICIANS
13140 Coit Road, LB 144
Dallas, TX 75240

OPTICIANS ASSOCIATIONS OF AMERICA
10341 Democracy Lane
P.O. Box 10110
Fairfax, VA 22030

OPTOMETRIST

Examines eyes to determine visual efficiency and performance, diseases, or other abnormalities by means of instrumentation and observation, and prescribes corrective procedures: Conserves, improves, and corrects vision through use of lenses, prisms, vision therapy, visual training, and control of visual environment. Examines patients for visual pathology or ocular manifestations of systemic disease, and refers those with pathological conditions to medical practitioner for further diagnosis and treatment. May specialize in treatment of children with learning problems, vision of aged, rehabilitation of partially sighted, or environmental vision. May specialize in vision training, vision therapy, vision development, contact lenses, or low vision aids. May conduct research, instruct in college or university, act as consultant, or work in public health field.

AMERICAN ACADEMY OF OPTOMETRY
5530 Wisconsin Avenue, NW, Suite 745
Washington, DC 20815

AMERICAN OPTOMETRIC ASSOCIATION
243 North Lindbergh Boulevard
St. Louis, MO 63141

ASSOCIATION OF SCHOOLS & COLLEGES OF OPTOMETRY
6110 Executive Boulevard, Suite 514
Rockville, MD 20852

NATIONAL ASSOCIATION OF OPTOMETRISTS & OPTICIANS
18903 South Miles Road
Cleveland, OH 44128

ORTHOTIST

Provides care to patients with disabling conditions of limbs and spine by fitting and preparing devices known as orthoses, under direction of and in consultation with PHYSICIAN: Assists in formulating of specifications for orthoses. Examines and evaluates patient's orthotic needs in relation to disease entity and functional loss. Formulates design of orthosis. Selects materials, making cast measurements, model modifications, and layouts. Performs fitting, including static and dynamic alinements. Evaluates orthosis on patient and makes adjustments to assure fit, function, cosmetics, and quality of work. Instructs patient in orthosis use. Maintains patient records. May supervise ORTHOTICS ASSISTANTS and other support personnel. May supervise laboratory activities relating to development of orthoses. May lecture and demonstrate to colleagues and other professionals concerned with orthotics. May participate in research. May perform functions of PROSTHETIST and be designated ORTHOTIST-PROSTHETIST.

AMERICAN ACADEMY OF ORTHOTISTS & PROSTHETISTS
717 Pendleton Street
Alexandria, VA 22314

OSTEOPATHIC PHYSICIAN

Diagnoses, prescribes for, and treats diseases of human body, relying upon accepted medical and surgical modalities: Examines patient to determine symptoms attributable to impairments in musculoskeletal system. Corrects disorders and affections of bones, muscles, nerves, and other body systems by medicinal and, surgical procedures and when deemed beneficial, manipulative therapy. Employs X-rays, drugs, and other aids to diagnose and treat bodily impairments. May practice any of known medical and surgical specialities.

AMERICAN COLLEGE OF GENERAL PRACTITIONERS & OSTEOPATHIC MEDICINE & SURGERY
2045 South Arlington Heights Road #104
Arlington Heights, IL 60005

AMERICAN OSTEOPATHIC ASSOCIATION
142 East Ontario Street
Chicago, IL 60611

STUDENT OSTEOPATHIC MEDICAL ASSOCIATION
National Office
4190 City Avenue
Philadelphia College of Osteopathic Medicine
Philadelphia, PA 19131

OTOLARYNGOLOGIST

Diagnoses and treats diseases of ear, nose, and throat: Examines affected organs, using equipment, such as audiometers, prisms, nasoscopes, microscopes, X-ray machines, and fluoroscopes. Determines nature and extent of disorder, and prescribes and administers medications or surgery. Performs tests to determine extent of disease or injury, prescribes and administers medications and immunizations, and performs variety of medical duties.

AMERICAN ACADEMY OF OTOLARYNGOLOGY-HEAD & NECK SURGERY
1101 Vermont Avenue, NW, Suite 302
Washington, DC 20005

PARAMEDIC

Administers first-aid treatment to and transports sick or injured persons to medical facility, working as member of emergency medical team: Responds to instructions from emergency medical dispatcher and drives specially equipped emergency vehicle to specified location. Monitors communication equipment to maintain contact with dispatcher. Removes or assists in removal of victims from scene of accident or catastrophe. Determines nature and extent of illness or injury, or magnitude of catastrophe, establishes first aid procedures to be followed or need for additional assistance, basing decisions on statements of persons involved, examination of victim or victims, and knowledge of emergency medical practice. Administers prescribed first-aid treatment at site of emergency, or in specially equipped vehicle, performing such activities as application of splints, administration of oxygen or intravenous injections, treatment of minor wounds or abrasions, or administration of artificial resuscitation. Communicates with professional medical personnel at emergency treatment facility to obtain instructions regarding further treatment and to arrange for reception of victims at treatment facility. Assists in removal of victims from vehicle and transfer of victims to treatment center. Assists treatment center admitting personnel to obtain and record information related to victims' vital statistics and circumstances of emergency. Maintains vehicles and medical and communication equipment and replenishes first-aid equipment and supplies. May assist in controlling crowds, protecting valuables, or performing other duties at scene of catastrophe. May assist professional medical personnel in emergency treatment administered at medical facility.

NATIONAL ASSOCIATION OF EMERGENCY MEDICAL TECHNICIANS
9140 Ward Park
Kansas City, MO 64114

PATHOLOGIST

Studies nature, cause, and development of diseases, and structural and functional changes caused by them: Diagnoses, from body tissue, fluids, secretions, and other specimens, presence and stage of disease, utilizing laboratory procedures. Acts as consultant to other medical practitioner. Performs autopsies to determine nature and extend of disease, cause of death, and effects of treatment. May direct activities of pathology department in medical school, hospital, clinic, medical examiner's office, or research institute. May be designated according to speciality as CLINICAL PATHOLOGIST; FORENSIC PATHOLOGIST; NEUROPATHOLOGIST; SURGICAL PATHOLOGIST.

AMERICAN SOCIETY OF CLINICAL PATHOLOGISTS
2100 West Harrison
Chicago, IL 60612

COLLEGE OF AMERICAN PATHOLOGISTS
5202 Old Orchard Road
Skokie, IL 60077

PEDIATRICIAN

Plans and carries out medical care program for children from birth through adolescence to aid in mental and physical growth and development: Examines patients to determine presence of disease and to establish preventative health practices. Ascertains nature and extent of disease or injury, prescribes and administers medications and immunizations, and performs variety of medical duties.

AMERICAN ACADEMY OF PEDIATRICS
141 West Point Boulevard
P.O. Box 927
Elk Grove Village, IL 60009

PERFUSIONIST

Sets up and operates heart-lung machine in hospital to take over functions of patient's heart and lungs during surgery or respiratory failure: Consults with surgeon or physician to obtain patient information needed to set up heart-lung machine. Assembles, sets up, and tests heart-lung machine to ensure that machine functions according to specifications. Operates heart-lung machine to regulate blood circulation and composition and oxygen and carbon dioxide levels, to administer drugs, and to control body temperature during surgery or respiratory failure of patient. Changes quantities administered at direction of physician, surgeon, or anesthesiologist. Cleans, repairs, and adjusts malfunctioning parts of heart-lung machine.

AMERICAN MEDICAL TECHNOLOGISTS
710 Higgins Road
Park Ridge, IL 60068

PHARMACIST

Compounds and dispenses medications, following prescriptions issued by PHYSICIAN; DENTIST; or other authorized medical practitioner: Weighs, measures, and mixes drugs and other medicinal compounds, and fills bottles or capsules with correct quantity and composition of preparation. Dispenses nonprescription medication to public. Advises self-diagnosing and self-medicating patients, or provides information on potential drug interactions, potential adverse drug reactions, and elements of patient's history which might bear on prescribing decision when in advisory capacity to PHYSICIAN. Advises patient regarding storage for prescription medication. Assures that patient understands prescribed instructions. Answers patient's questions regarding prescription medication. Stores and preserves biologicals, vaccines, serums, and other drugs subject to deterioration, utilizing refrigeration and other methods. Orders and maintains supply of drugs, chemicals, and other pharmaceutical stock. Insures specified quantity and potency of materials for medical use. May act as consultant to civic groups and health practitioner on matters pertaining to pharmacy. May assay medications to determine identity, purity, and strength. May instruct INTERNS and other medical personnel on matters pertaining to pharmacy, or teach in college of pharmacy. May work in particular area and be designated PHARMACIST, COMMUNITY; PHARMACIST, HOSPITAL.

AMERICAN ASSOCIATIONS OF COLLEGES OF PHARMACY
1426 Prince Street
Alexandria, VA 22314

AMERICAN FOUNDATION OF PHARMACEUTICAL EDUCATION
Radburn Plaza Building
14-25 Plaza Road
Fairlawn, NJ 07410

AMERICAN PHARMACEUTICAL ASSOCIATION
2215 Constitution Avenue, NW
Washington, DC 20037

AMERICAN SOCIETY OF CONSULTANT PHARMACISTS
2300 Ninth Street South
Arlington, VA 22204

AMERICAN SOCIETY OF HOSPITAL PHARMACISTS
4630 Montgomery Avenue
Bethesda, MD 20814

PHLEBOTOMIST

Draws blood from patients or donors in hospital, blood bank, or similar facility for analysis or other medical purposes: Assembles equipment, such as tourniquet, needles, blood collection devices, gauze, cotton, and alcohol on work tray, according to requirements for specified tests or procedures. Verifies or records identity of patient or donor and converses with patient or donor to allay fear of procedure. Applies tourniquet to arm, locates accessible vein, swabs puncture area with disinfectant, and inserts needle into vein to draw blood into collection tube or bag. Withdraws needle, applies treatment to puncture site, and labels and stores blood container for subsequent processing. May prick finger to draw blood.

May conduct interviews, take vital signs, and draw and test blood samples to screen donors at blood bank.

NATIONAL PHLEBOTOMY ASSOCIATION
2623 Bladensburgh Road, NE
Washington, DC 20018

PHYSIATRIST

Specializes in clinical and diagnostic use of physical agents and exercises to provide physiotherapy for physical, mental, and occupational rehabilitation of patients: Examines patient, utilizing electrodiagnosis and other diagnostic procedures to determine need for and extent of therapy. Prescribes and administers treatment, using therapeutic methods and procedures, such as light therapy, diathermy, electrosurkineistherapy. Instructs PHYSICAL THERAPIST and other personnel in nature and duration or dosage of treatment, and determines that treatments are administered properly. Prescribes exercises designed to develop functions of specific anatomical parts or specific muscle groups. Recommends occupational therapy activities for patients with extended convalescent periods and for those whose disability requires change of occupation.

ASSOCIATION OF ACADEMIC PHYSIATRISTS
8000 Five Mile Road, Suite 340
Cincinnati, OH 45230

PHYSICAL THERAPIST

Plans and administers medically prescribed physical therapy, treatment programs for patients to restore function, relieve pain, and prevent disability following disease, injury, or loss of body part, working at hospital, rehabilitation center, nursing home, home-health agency, or in private practice: Reviews and evaluates PHYSICIAN'S referral (prescription) and patient's medical records to determine physical therapy treatment required. Performs patient tests, measurements and evaluations, such as range-of-motion and manual-muscle tests, gait and functional analyses, and body-parts measurements, and records and evaluates findings to aid in establishing or revising specifics of treatment programs. Plans and prepares written treatment program based on evaluation of available patient data. Administers manual therapeutic exercises to improve or maintain muscle function, applying precise amounts of muscle force and guiding patient's body parts through selective patterns and degrees of movement. Instructs, motivates, and assists patients in nonmanual exercises, such as active regimens, isometric, and progressive-resistive, and in functional activities, such as ambulation, transfer, and daily-living activities, using weights, pulleys, exercise machines, mats, steps, and inclined surfaces, and assistive and supportive devices, such as crutches, canes, parallel bars, orthoses, and prostheses. Administers treatments involving application of physical agents, such as light, heat, water, and electricity, using equipment such as hydrotherapy tanks and whirlpool baths, moist packs, ultraviolet and infrared lamps, low-voltage generators, and diathermy and ultrasound machines; evaluates effects of treatments at various intensities and durations and adjusts treatments to achieve maximum benefit. Administers massage, applying deep and superficial massage techniques. Administers traction to relieve neck and back pain, using intermittent and static traction equipment. Records patient treatment, response, and progress. Instructs patient and family in physical therapy procedures to be continued at home. Evaluates, fits, and adjusts prosthetic and orthotic devices and recommends modifications to ORTHOTIST. Confers with PHYSICIAN and other health practitioners to obtain additional patient information, suggest revisions in treatment program, and integrate physical therapy treatment with other aspects of patient health care. Orients, instructs, and directs work activities of PHYSICAL THERAPIST ASSISTANTS or PHYSICAL THERAPY AIDES. May plan and conduct lectures and training programs on physical therapy and related topics for medical staff, students, and community groups. May train and evaluate clinical students. May plan and develop physical therapy research programs and participate in conducting research. May write technical articles and reports for publications. May teach physical therapy techniques and procedures in educational institutions. May limit treatment to specific patient group or disability and be designated PHYSICAL THERAPIST, PEDIATRIC; PHYSICAL THERAPIST, PULMONARY; or specialize in conducting physical therapy research and be designated PHYSICAL THERAPIST RESEARCH. In facilities where Physical Therapist Assistants are also employed, PHYSICAL THERAPISTS may primarily administer complex treatments, such as certain types of manual exercise and functional training, and monitor administration of other treatments.

AMERICAN PHYSICAL THERAPY ASSOCIATION
1111 North Fairfax Street
Alexandria, VA 22314

PODIATRIST

Diagnoses and treats diseases and deformities of human foot: Diagnoses foot ailments, such as tumors, ulcers, fractures, skin or nail diseases, and congenital or acquired deformities, utilizing diagnostic aids, such as urinalysis, blood tests, and X-ray analysis. Treats deformities, such as flat or weak feet and foot imbalance, by mechanical and electrical methods, such as whirlpool or raraffin baths and short wave and low voltage currents. Treats conditions, such as corns, calluses, ingrowing nails, tumors, shortened tendons, bunions, cysts, and abscesses by surgical methods, including suturing, medications, and administration of local anesthetics. Prescribes drugs. Does not perform foot amputations. Corrects deformities by means of plaster casts and strappings. Makes and fits prosthetic appliances. Prescribes corrective footwear. Advises patients concerning continued treatment of disorders and proper foot care to prevent recurrence. Refers patients to PHYSICIAN when symptoms observed in feet and legs indicate systemic disorders, such as arthritis, heart disease, diabetes, or kidney trouble. May treat bone, muscle, and joint disorders and be designated PODIATRIST, ORTHOPEDIC; childrens' foot diseases and be designated PODOPEDIATRICIAN, or perform surgery and be designated PODIATRIC SURGEON.

AMERICAN ASSOCIATION OF COLLEGES OF PODIATRIC MEDICINE
6110 Executive Boulevard, Suite 204
Rockville, MD 20852

NATIONAL PODIATRIC MEDICAL ASSOCIATION
c/o Raymond E. Lee
1638 East 87th Street
Chicago, IL 60617

PROCTOLOGIST

Diagnoses and treats diseases and disorders of anus, rectum, and colon: Diagnoses diseases and disorders utilizing techniques, such as discussion of symptoms and medical history with patient, instrumental inspection of rectum and colon, examination of X-ray photographs of affected parts, and evaluation of laboratory test results. Treats diseases and disorders by surgical removal or repair of diseased or malfunctioning parts, or by prescription of appropriate medication and suggestions for adaptation of patient's living habits.

AMERICAN SOCIETY OF COLON & RECTAL SURGEONS
615 Griswold, #1717
Detroit, MI 44826

INTERNATIONAL ACADEMY OF PROCTOLOGY
c/o George Donnally, M.D.
1203 Hadley Road
Mooresville, IN 46158

PROSTHETIST

Provides care to patients with partial or total absence of limb by planning fabrication of, writing specifications for, and fitting devices known as prosthesis under guidance of and in consultation with PHYSICIAN: Assists PHYSICIAN in formulation of prescription. Examines and evaluates patient's prosthetic needs in relation to disease entity and functional loss. Formulates design of prosthesis and selects materials and components. Makes casts, measurements, and model modifications. Performs fitting, including static and dynamic alinements. Evaluates prosthesis on patient and makes adjustments to assure fit, function, comfort, and workmanship. Instructs patient in prosthesis use. Maintains patient records. May supervise PROSTHETICS ASSISTANTS and other personnel. May supervise laboratory activities relating to development of prosthesis. May lecture and demonstrate to colleagues and other professionals concerned with practice of prosthetics. May participate in research. May also perform functions of ORTHOTIST.

AMERICAN ACADEMY OF ORTHOTISTS & PROSTHETISTS
717 Pendleton Street
Alexandria, VA 22314

PSYCHIATRIST

Studies, diagnoses, and treats mental, emotional, and behavioral disorders: Organizes data concerning patient's family, personal (medical and mental) history, and onset of symptoms obtained from patient, relatives, and other sources, such as NURSE. Examines patient to determine general physical condition, following standard medical procedures. Orders laboratory and other special diagnostic tests and evaluates data obtained. Determines nature and extent of mental disorder, and formulates treatment program. Treats or directs treatment of patient, utilizing somatic, group, and milieu therapy, and variety of psychotherapeutic methods and medications.

AMERICAN BOARD OF PSYCHIATRY & NEUROLOGY
500 Lake Cook Road, Suite 335
Deerfield, IL 60015

AMERICAN PSYCHIATRIC ASSOCIATION
1400 K Street, NW
Washington, DC 2005

ORTHOPSYCHIATRIC ASSOCIATION
19 West 44th Street, #1616
New York, NY 10036

PULMONARY FUNCTION TECHNICIAN

Performs pulmonary function, lung-capacity, and blood-and-oxygen tests to gather data for medical evaluation, following instructions of supervisor: Confers with patient in treatment room to explain test procedures. Explains specified methods of breathing to patient and conducts pulmonary-function tests, such as helium dilution and gross spirometry tests, and lung-capacity tests, such as vital capacity and maximum breathing capacity tests, using spirometer. Activates co-oximeter and injects blood specimen into co-oximeter to perform blood analysis tests, such as oxygen saturation and red cell count. Collects and analyzes contents of expired air of patient, using oxygen analyzer. Observes and records readings on metering devices of analysis equipment, and conveys findings of tests and analyses to supervisor for evaluation.

NATIONAL SOCIETY FOR CARDIOVASCULAR & PULMONARY TECHNOLOGY
1133 15th Street, NW, Suite 1000
Washington, DC 20005

RADIATION THERAPY TECHNOLOGIST

Operates radiation therapy equipment to treat patients with prescribed doses of ionizing radiation: Positions patient under equipment to expose necessary areas to treatment and adjust equipment according to instructions. Calculates exposure time and intensity required, using mechanical and electronic regulating controls. Turns controls to operate and adjust equipment and regulate application. Observes dials to monitor duration and intensity of treatment. Prepares and maintains records for review by medical staff.

AMERICAN MEDICAL TECHNOLOGISTS
710 Higgins Road
Park Ridge, IL 60068

RADIOLOGIC TECHNOLOGIST

Applies roentgen rays and radioactive substances to patients for diagnostic and therapeutic purposes: Positions patient under X-ray machine, adjusts immobilization devices, and affixes lead plates to protect unaffected areas. Administers drugs or chemical mixtures orally or as enemas to render organs opaque. Adjusts switches regulating length and intensity of exposure. Assists in treating diseased or affected areas of body, under supervision of PHYSICIAN, by exposing area to specified concentrations of X-rays for prescribed periods of time. Prepares reports and maintains records of services rendered. Makes minor adjustments to equipment. May assist in therapy requiring application of radium or radioactive isotopes. May specialize in taking X-rays of specific areas of body.

AMERICAN MEDICAL TECHNOLOGISTS
710 Higgins Road
Park Ridge, IL 60068

RADIOLOGIST

Diagnoses and treats diseases of human body, using X-rays and radioactive substances: Examines internal structures and functions of organ systems, making diagnoses after correlation of X-ray findings with other examinations and tests. Treats benign and malignant internal and external growths by exposure to radiation from X-rays, high energy sources, and natural and manmade radioisotopes directed at or implanted in affected areas of body. Administers radiopaque substances by injection, orally, or as enemas to render internal structures and organs visible on X-ray films or fluoroscopic screens. May specialize in diagnostic radiology or radiation therapy. May diagnose and treat diseases of human body, using radionuclides (radioisotopes) and be designated DOCTOR OF NUCLEAR MEDICINE.

AMERICAN COLLEGE OF RADIOLOGY
1891 Preston White Drive
Reston, VA 22091

AMERICAN REGISTRY OF RADIOLOGIC TECHNOLOGISTS
2600 Wayzata Boulevard
Minneapolis, MN 55405

AMERICAN SOCIETY OF RADIOLOGIC TECHNOLOGISTS
15000 Central Avenue, SE
Albuquerque, NM 87123

RADIOPHARMACIST

Prepares and dispenses radioactive pharmaceuticals used for patient diagnosis and therapy, applying principles and practices of pharmacy and radiochemistry: Receives radiopharmaceutical prescription from PHYSICIAN and reviews prescription to determine suitability of radiopharmaceutical for intended use. Verifies that specified radioactive substance and reagent will give desired results in examination or treatment procedures, utilizing knowledge of radiopharmaceutical preparation and principles of drug biodistribution. Calculates volume of radioactive pharmaceutical required to provide patient with desired level of radioactivity at prescribed time, according to established rates of radioisotope decay. Compounds radioactive substances and reagents to prepare radiopharmaceutical, following radiopharmacy laboratory procedures. Assays prepared radiopharmaceutical, using measuring and analysis instruments and equipment, such as ionization chamber, pulse-height analyzer, and radioisotope does calibrator, to verify rate of drug disintegration and to ensure that patient receives required dose. Consults with PHYSICIAN following patient treatment of procedure to review and evaluate quality and effectiveness of radiopharmaceutical. Conducts research to develop or improve radiopharmaceuticals. Prepares reports for regulatory agencies to obtain approval for testing and use of new radiopharmaceuticals. Maintains control records for receipt, storage, preparation, and disposal of radioactive nuclei. Occasionally conducts training for students and medical professionals concerning radiopharmacy use, characteristics, and compounding procedures.

AMERICAN ASSOCIATIONS OF COLLEGES OF PHARMACY
1426 Prince Street
Alexandria, VA 22314

AMERICAN FOUNDATION OF PHARMACEUTICAL EDUCATION
Radburn Plaza Building
14-25 Plaza Road
Fairlawn, NJ 07410

AMERICAN PHARMACEUTICAL ASSOCIATION
2215 Constitution Avenue, NW
Washington, DC 20037

AMERICAN SOCIETY OF CONSULTANT PHARMACISTS
2300 Ninth Street South
Arlington, VA 22204

AMERICAN SOCIETY OF HOSPITAL PHARMACISTS
4630 Montgomery Avenue
Bethesda, MD 20814

RESPIRATORY THERAPIST

Administers respiratory therapy care and life support to patients with deficiencies and abnormalities of cardiopulmonary system, under supervision of PHYSICIAN and by prescription: Sets up and operates devices, such as respirators, mechanical ventilators, therapeutic gas administration apparatus, environmental control systems, and aerosol generators. Observes equipment gages to insure specified volumes are maintained. Performs bronchopulmonary drainage and assists patient in performing breathing exercises. Monitors patient's physiological responses to therapy, as well as equipment function. Consults with PHYSICIAN in event of adverse reactions. Maintains patient's chart that contains pertinent identification and therapy information. Inspects and tests respiratory therapy equipment to insure proper operating condition. Orders major repairs when needed. May demonstrate respirator care procedures to trainees and other health care personnel.

AMERICAN ASSOCIATION FOR RESPIRATORY CARE
1720 Regal Row
Dallas, TX 75235

AMERICAN MEDICAL TECHNOLOGISTS
710 Higgins Road
Park Ridge, IL 60068

SPEECH PATHOLOGIST

Specializes in diagnosis and treatment of speech and language problems, and engages in scientific study of human communication: Diagnoses and evaluates speech and language competencies of individuals, including assessment of speech and language skills as related to educational, medical, social, and psychological factors. Plans, directs, or conducts habilitative and rehabilitative treatment programs to restore communicative efficiency of individuals with communication problems of organic and nonorganic etiology. Provides counseling and guidance to speech and language handicapped individuals. May act as consultant to educational, medical, and other professional groups. May teach scientific principles of human communication. May direct scientific projects investigating biophysical and biosocial phenomena associated with voice, speech, and language. May conduct research to develop diagnostic and remedial techniques or design apparatus. See AUDIOLOGIST for one who specializes in diagnosis of, and provision of rehabilitative services for, auditory problems.

COUNCIL ON PROFESSIONAL STANDARDS IN SPEECH-LANGUAGE PATHOLOGY AND AUDIOLOGY
American Speech-Language-Hearing Association
10801 Rockville Pike
Rockville, MD 20852

SURGEON

Performs surgery to correct deformities, repair injuries, prevent diseases, and improve function in patients: Examines patient to verify necessity of operation, estimate possible risk to patient, and determine best operational procedure. Reviews reports of patient's general physical condition, reactions to medications, and medical history. Examines instruments, equipment, and surgical setup to insure that antiseptic and aseptic methods have been followed. Performs operations, using variety of surgical instruments and employing established surgical techniques appropriate for specific procedures. May specialize in particular type of operation, as on nervous system, and be designated NEUROSURGEON. May specialize in skin grafts and bone and tissue transplants to restore or repair damaged, lost or deformed parts of face and body, and be designated PLASTIC SURGEON. May specialize in correction or prevention of skeletal abnormalities utilizing surgical, medical, and physical methodologies and be designated ORTHOPEDIC SURGEON.

AMERICAN COLLEGE OF SURGEONS
55 East Erie Street
Chicago, IL 60611

AMERICAN ORTHOPEDIC FOOT & ANKLE SOCIETY
222 South Prospect Avenue
Park Ridge, IL 60068

SURGICAL TECHNICIAN

Performs any combination of following tasks before, during, and after operation: Washes, shaves, and sterilizes operative area of patient. Scrubs hands and dons cap, mask, gown, and rubber gloves. Places equipment and supplies in operating room according to SURGEON'S directions, and arranges instruments as specified by NURSE, GENERAL DUTY. Aids team to don gowns and gloves. Maintains specified supply of such fluids as plasma, saline, blood, and glucose for use during operation. Adjusts lights and other equipment as directed. Washes and sterilizes used equipment, using germicides, autoclave, and sterilizer. Cleans operating room. Counts sponges, needles, and instruments used during operation. May assist in administering blood, plasma, or other injections and transfusions. May hand SURGEON instruments and supplies, hold retractors, and cut sutures, as directed during operation.

AMERICAN ASSOCIATION OF SURGEONS ASSISTANTS
1980 Isaac Newton Square South
Reston, VA 22090

AMERICAN MEDICAL TECHNOLOGISTS
710 Higgins Road
Park Ridge, IL 60068

TISSUE TECHNOLOGIST

Cuts, stains, mounts, and prepares tissues for examination by PATHOLOGIST: Prepares specimen for immediate analysis by freezing. Decalcifies bone specimens. Prepares and maintains paraffin, reagents, and other solutions and stains, according to standard formulas. May assist PATHOLOGIST in autopsy.

AMERICAN MEDICAL TECHNOLOGISTS
710 Higgins Road
Park Ridge, IL 60068

ULTRASOUND TECHNOLOGIST

Operates ultrasound diagnostic equipment to produce two-dimensional ultrasonic pattern and positive pictures of internal organs, for use by professional personnel in diagnosis of disease, study of malfunction of organs, and prenatal examination of fetus and placenta: Selects equipment for use in ultrasound setup according to specifications of examination. Explains process to patient, and instructs and assists patient in assuming physical position for required exposure to ultrasonic waves. Adjusts equipment controls according to specific orders and part of body to be examined. Moves transducer by hand or by manipulation of remote control device and observes sound wave display screen to note ultrasonic pattern produced. Activates equipment which automatically produces visual image of internal organs from ultrasonic pattern, or which produces continuing recorder strip printout of ultrasonic pattern. Photographs visual image of organs shown on display module, or removes recorder strip printout from machine when specified time for recording has elapsed, to obtain permanent record of internal examination. Attaches identification tag to photographs or recorder printouts to insure maintenance of records. Discusses test results with department supervisor or professional personnel to determine whether additional ultrasound examination is required, and repeats process as needed to secure desired results.

AMERICAN REGISTRY OF DIAGNOSTIC MEDICAL SONOGRAPHERS
32 East Hollister Street
Cincinnati, OH 45219

SOCIETY OF DIAGNOSTIC MEDICAL SONOGRAPHERS
P.O. Box 741415
Dallas, TX 75234

UROLOGIST

Diagnoses and treats diseases and disorders of genitourinary organs and tract: Examines patient, using X-ray machine, fluoroscope, and other equipment to aid in determining nature and extent of disorder or injury. Treats patient, using diathermy machine, catheter, systoscope, radium emanation tube, and similar equipment. Performs surgery, as indicated. Prescribes and administers urinary antiseptics to combat infection.

AMERICAN UROLOGICAL ASSOCIATION ALLIED
1120 North Charles Street
Baltimore, MD 21201

UTILIZATION REVIEW COORDINATOR

Supervises and coordinates activities of utilization review staff and develops policies, standards, and procedures governing admissions and treatment of patients of health care facility: Analyzes individual patient records to determine legitimacy of admission and continued stay in health care facility, reviews patient treatment plans to ensure adherence to established criteria and standards, and supervises activities of utilization review staff. Reviews and analyzes governmental and accrediting agency standards governing admissions, treatment, and continued stay of patients to develop policies, procedures, and criteria for facility center. Reviews application for patient admission and determines necessity of each admission, applying established admission criteria. Approves admission or refers case to facility Utilization Review Committee for review and course of action when case fails to meet criteria. Reviews inpatient medical records to determine necessity of continued stay or discharge. Reviews physician treatment plans for inpatients to determine appropriateness of plan to patient manifested conditions and to ensure consistency with standard medical practice and facility policies. Makes clinical judgement regarding correctness of physician directed care. Determines next review date in accordance with established diagnostic criteria. Abstracts data from records. Assists review committee in planning and holding federally mandated quality assurance reviews, periodic medical reviews, and professional reviews. Serves as review committee liaison with other committees within facility in development of policies and procedures. Participates in facility orientation and training programs. Supervises and coordinates activities of utilization review staff in maintenance of policy and procedure manuals, file, records, and correspondence.

AMERICAN COLLEGE OF UTILIZATION REVIEW PHYSICIANS
Southbridge Park, Building 3, Suite 304
1521 Tamiami Trail
Venice, FL 34292

NATIONAL ASSOCIATION OF QUALITY ASSURANCE PROFESSIONALS
104 Wilmont, Suite 201
Dearfield, IL 60015

VOICE PATHOLOGIST

Diagnoses and treats voice disorders, such as those associated with professional use of voice: Develops and implements perceptual evaluation procedures and psychophysical methods of voice assessment. Collects diagnostic data on individuals, such as output pressures, airflow, chestwall movements, and articular and laryngeal displacement, using scopes and other measuring instruments. Analyzes and interprets diagnostic data and consults with OTOLARYNGOLOGIST and other professionals to determine method or treatment, such as surgery, vocal modification, or voice therapy. Plans and conducts voice therapy sessions, applying auditory, visual, kinematic, and biofeedback techniques. Plans and conducts voice hygiene workshops. Calibrates equipment. May teach voice science to associates and direct research in area of voice. May establish procedures and direct operation of laboratory specializing in diagnosing and treating voice disorders.

COUNCIL ON PROFESSIONAL STANDARDS IN SPEECH-LANGUAGE PATHOLOGY AND AUDIOLOGY
American Speech-Language-Hearing Association
10801 Rockville Pike
Rockville, MD 20852

PAWNBROKER

PAWNBROKER

Estimates pawn or pledge value of articles, such as jewelry, cameras, and musical instruments, and lends money to customer: Examines article to determine condition and worth. Weighs gold or silver articles on coin scales or employs acid tests to determine carat content and purity to verify value of articles. Inspects diamonds and other gems for flaws and color, using loupe (magnifying glass). Assigns pledge value to article based on knowledge of values or listing of wholesale prices. Rejects articles in unsatisfactory condition or having no pledge value. Issues pledge tickets and keeps record of loans. Computes interest when pledges are redeemed or extended. Sells unredeemed pledge items. May examine customer's identification and record thumbprints for police reports. May testify in court proceedings involving stolen merchandise.

AMERICAN PAWNBROKERS ASSOCIATION
Box 2043
St. George, UT 84770

PERSONNEL

BENEFITS MANAGER

Manages employee benefits program for establishment: Plans and directs implementation and administration of benefits programs designed to insure employees against loss of income because of illness, injury, layoff, or retirement. Directs preparation and distribution of informational literature and verbal presentations to notify and advise employees of eligibility for benefits programs, such as insurance plans, paid time off, bonus pay, and special employer-sponsored activities. Analyzes company benefits policies, laws concerning mandatory insurance coverage, data concerning prevailing practices among similar organizations, and agreements with labor unions, in order to comply with legal requirements and to establish competitive benefits programs. Modifies aspects of existing program according to findings, utilizing knowledge of prevailing practices, emerging types of benefits packages, and customary benefits provided for production, supervisory, and executive personnel. Directs performance of clerical functions, such as updating records and processing insurance claims.

EMPLOYEE BENEFIT RESEARCH INSTITUTE
2121 K Street, NW, Suite 860
Washington, DC 20037

INTERNATIONAL FOUNDATION OF EMPLOYEE BENEFIT PLANS
18700 Bluemound Road
Brookfield, WI 53005

EMPLOYMENT INTERVIEWERS

Employment interviewers, are also called account representatives, manpower development specialists, counselors, or personnel consultants. They help jobseekers find employment and help employers find qualified staff. They work in private personnel consultant firms or state employment security offices (also known as job service centers). They act as brokers, putting together the best combination of applicant and job. To accomplish this, they obtain information from employers as well as jobseekers. Employers generally pay private (but not public) agencies for finding them workers. Either way, the employer places a "job order" with the firm that describes the opening and lists requirements such as education, licenses or credentials, and experience. Once an appropriate type of job has been identified, the employment interviewer searches the file of job orders seeking a possible job match, and refers the applicant to the employer. Some employment interviewers work in temporary help service companies that need temporary help.

ASSOCIATION OF EXECUTIVE SEARCH CONSULTANTS
151 Railroad Avenue
Greenwich, CT 06830

EMPLOYMENT MANAGEMENT ASSOCIATION
20 William Street
Wellesley, MA 02181

NATIONAL ASSOCIATION OF PERSONNEL CONSULTANTS
1432 Duke Street
Alexandria, VA 22314

NATIONAL PERSONNEL CONSULTANTS
535 Court Street
P.O. Box 1379
Reading, PA 19603

PERSONNEL MANAGER

Plans and carries out policies relating to all phases of personnel activity: Recruits, interviews, and selects employees to fill vacant positions. Plans and conducts new employee orientation to foster positive attitude toward company goals. Keeps record of insurance coverage, pension plan, and personnel transactions, such as hires, promotions, transfers, and terminations. Investigates accidents and prepares reports for insurance carrier. Conducts wage survey within labor market to determine competitive wage rate. Prepares budget of personnel operatings.

Meets with shop stewards and supervisors to resolve grievances. Writes separation notices for employees separating with cause and conducts exit interviews to determine reasons behind separations. Prepares reports and recommends procedures to reduce absenteeism and turnover. May keep records of hired employee characteristics for governmental reporting purposes. May negotiate collective bargaining agreement with BUSINESS REPRESENTATIVE, LABOR UNION.

AMERICAN SOCIETY FOR PERSONNEL ADMINISTRATION
606 North Washington Street
Alexandria, VA 22314

PEST CONTROL

EXTERMINATOR
Sprays chemical solutions or toxic gases and sets mechanical traps to kill pests that infest buildings and surrounding areas: Fumigates rooms and buildings, using toxic gases. Sprays chemical solutions or dust powders in rooms and work areas. Places poisonous paste or bait and mechanical traps where pests are present. May clean areas that harbor pests, using rakes, brooms, shovels, and mops preparatory to fumigating. May be required to hold state license. May be designated according to type of pest eliminated as RODENT EXTERMINATOR.

ELECTRONIC PEST CONTROL ASSOCIATION
710 East Ogden, Suite 114
Naperville, IL 60540

INTERNATIONAL PESTICIDE APPLICATORS ASSOCIATION
P.O. Box 1377
Milton, WA 98354

NATIONAL PEST CONTROL ASSOCIATION
8100 Oak Street
Dunn Loring, VA 22027

PLUMBING MAINTENANCE

PLUMBER, MAINTENANCE
Assembles, installs, and repairs pipes, fittings, and fixtures of heating, water, and drainage systems, according to specifications and plumbing codes: Studies

building plans and working drawings to determine work aids required and sequence of installations. Inspects structure to ascertain obstructions to be avoided to prevent weakening of structure resulting from installation of pipe. Locates and marks position of pipe and pipe connections and passage holes for pipes in walls and floors, using ruler, spirit level, and plumb bob. Cuts openings in walls and floors to accommodate pipe and pipe fittings, usings handtools and power tools. Cuts and threads pipe, using pipe cutters, cutting torch, and pipe-threading machine. Bends pipe to required angle by use of pipe-bending machine or by placing pipe over block and bending it by hand. Assembles and installs valves, pipe fittings, and pipes composed of metals, such as iron, steel, brass, and lead, and nonmetals, such as glass, vitrified clay, and plastic, using handtools and power tools. Joins pipes by use of screws, bolts, fittings, solder, plastic solvent, and calks joints. Fills pipe system with water or air and reads pressure gages to determine whether system is leaking. Installs and repair plumbing fixtures, such as sinks, commodes, bathtubs, water heaters, hot water tanks, garbage disposal units, dishwashers, and water softeners. Repairs and maintains plumbing, by replacing washers in leaky faucets, mending burst pipes, and opening clogged drains. May weld holding fixtures to steel structural members.

AMERICAN SOCIETY OF PLUMBING ENGINEERS
3617 Thousand Oaks Boulevard, Suite 210
West Lake, CA 91362

NATIONAL ASSOCIATION OF PLUMBING-HEATING-COOLING CONTRACTORS
P.O. Box 6808
180 South Washington Street
Falls Church, VA 22046

UNITED ASSOCIATION OF JOURNEYMEN & APPRENTICES OF THE PLUMBING & PIPE FITTING INDUSTRY OF THE U.S. & CANADA
P.O. Box 37800
Washington, DC 20013

SEWER PIPE CLEANER
Removes roots, debris, and other refuse from clogged sewer lines and drains, using portable electric sewer cleaning machine, and repairs breaks in underground piping: Positions or disassembles sewer trap machine at sewer or drain outlet. Removes drain cover, using wrench. Installs rotary knives on flexible cable, mounted on reel of machine, according to diameter of pipe to be cleaned. Starts machine to feed revolving cable into opening, stopping machine and changing knives as necessary to conform to diameter or contour of pipe. Withdraws cable to deposit accumulated residue removed from pipe in containers for disposal. Observes residue for evidence of mud, indicating broken sewer line. Measures distance from sewer opening to suspected break, using plumbers' snake, tape line, or by estimating position of cutting head within sewer. Notifies co-workers to dig

out ruptured line or digs out shallow sewers, using shovel. Removes and replaces broken tile section or pipe, using calking compound and cement to form watertight joint. Replaces or directs replacement of earth. Replaces dull knives and performs repairs on machine, using handtools. May estimate cost of service to customer. May clean sewage collection points and sanitary lines in streets and sewage plants.

NATIONAL ASSOCIATION OF PLUMBING-HEATING-COOLING CONTRACTORS
P.O. Box 6808
180 South Washington Street
Falls Church, VA 22046

PROPERTY MANAGEMENT

PROPERTY MANAGER

Manages commercial, industrial, or residential real estate properties for clients: Negotiates with client terms and conditions for providing management services, and drafts agreement stipulating extent and scope of management responsibilities, services to be performed, and costs for services. Prepares lease or rental agreements for lessees and collects specified rents and impounds. Directs bookkeeping functions, or credits client account for receipts and debits account for disbursements, such as mortgage, taxes, and insurance premium payments, management services costs, and upkeep and maintenance costs. Arranges for alterations to, or maintenance, upkeep, or reconditioning of property as specified in management services or lessee's agreement. Employs, or contracts for services of, security, maintenance, and groundskeeping personnel and onsite management personnel if required. Purchases supplies and equipment for use on leased properties. Directs preparation of financial statements and reports on status of properties, such as occupancy rates and dates of expiration of leases. Directs issuance of check for monies due client. May advise client relative to financing, purchasing, or selling of property. Usually required to have real estate broker's license and be certified in property management.

INSTITUTE OF REAL ESTATE MANAGEMENT
430 North Michigan Avenue
Chicago, IL 60611

NATIONAL ASSOCIATION OF REALTORS
430 North Michigan Avenue
Chicago, IL 60611

PSYCHOLOGY

PSYCHOLOGIST

Provides individual and group counseling services in universities and colleges, schools, clinics, rehabilitation centers, Veterans Administration hospitals, and industry, to assist individuals in achieving more effective personal, social, educational, and vocational development and adjustment: Collects data about individual through use of interview, case history, and observational techniques. Selects and interprets psychological tests designed to assess individual's intelligence, aptitudes, abilities, and interests, applying knowledge of statistical analysis. Evaluates data to identify causes of problem of individuals and to determine advisability of counseling or referral to other specialists or institutions. Conducts counseling or therapeutic interviews to assist individual to gain insight into personal problems, define goals, and plan action reflecting interests, abilities, and needs. Provides occupational, educational, and other information to enable individual to formulate realistic educational and vocational plans. Follows up results of counseling to determine reliability and validity of treatment used. May engage in research to develop and improve diagnostic and counseling techniques. May administer and score psychological tests.

> **AMERICAN PSYCHOLOGICAL ASSOCIATION**
> 1200 17th Street, NW
> Washington, DC 20036

RELIGION

CLERGY MEMBER

Conducts religious worship and performs other spiritual functions associated with beliefs and practices of religious faith or denomination as authorized, and provides spiritual and moral guidance and assistance to members: Leads congregation in worship services. Prepares and delivers sermons and other talks. Interprets doctrine of religion. Instructs people who seek conversion to faith. Conducts wedding and funeral services. Administers rites or ordinances of church. Visits sick and shut-ins, and helps poor. Counsels those in spiritual need and comforts bereaved. Oversees religious education programs, such as Sunday school and youth groups. May write articles for publication and engage in interfaith, community, civic, educational, and recreational activities sponsored by or related to interest of denomination. May teach in seminaries and universities. May serve in armed forces, institutions, or industry. May carry religious message and medical or educational aid to foreign lands and people to obtain converts and establish native church

NATIONAL COUNCIL OF CHURCHES OF CHRIST IN THE U.S.A.
Professional Church Leadership
475 Riverside Drive, Room 770
New York, NY 10115

NATIONAL CATHOLIC VOCATIONAL COUNCIL
1307 South Wabash Avenue
Chicago, IL 60605

THE JEWISH THEOLOGICAL SEMINARY OF AMERICA
3080 Broadway
New York, NY 10027

REPAIR AND MAINTENANCE

AIR-CONDITIONING, HEATING, AND REFRIGERATION REPAIRER

Air-conditioning, heating, and refrigeration mechanics are skilled workers who install, maintain, and repair such systems. Today, heating and air-conditioning systems control the temperature, humidity, and even the cleanliness of the air in homes, stores, offices, factories, and schools. In addition, refrigeration systems make it possible to store food, blood, and other perishable items. Furnace installers, also called heating equipment installers, follow blueprints or other specifications to install oil, gas, electric, solid-fuel, and multifuel heating systems. After setting the equipment in place, they often install fuel and water supply lines, air ducts and vents, pumps, and other components. They then connect electrical wiring and controls, and check the unit for proper operation. After a furnace has been installed, the mechanic must perform routine maintenance and repair in order to keep the system operating efficiently. During the fall and winter, when the system is needed most, they service and adjust burners. If the system is not operating properly, mechanics check the thermostat, burner nozzles, controls, and other parts to locate the problem. The mechanic corrects the problem by adjusting or replacing parts. During the summer, mechanics do maintenance work, such as replacing filters and vacuum-cleaning vents, ducts, and other parts of the heating system that may accumulate soot and ash if not adjusted properly. When air-conditioning and refrigeration equipment breaks down, mechanics diagnose the cause and make repairs. To find defects, they test parts such as compressors, relays, and thermostats. During the winter, air-conditioning mechanics inspect the systems and do required maintenance, such as overhauling compressors. Heating, air-conditioning, and refrigeration mechanics use a variety of tools, including hammers, wrenches, metal snips , electric drills, pipe cutters and benders, and acetylene torches, to work with refrigerant lines and air ducts. They use voltmeters, thermometers, pressure gauges, manometers, and other testing devices to check air flow, refrigerant pressures, electrical circuits, burners, and other components.

AIR CONDITIONING CONTRACTORS OF AMERICA
1228 17th Street, NW
Washington, DC 20036

AIR CONDITIONING & REFRIGERATION INSTITUTE
1510 Wilson Boulevard, 6th Floor
Arlington, VA 22209

COUNCIL OF AIR CONDITIONING AND REFRIGERATION INDUSTRY
c/o Melissa Woodring
Mechanical Contractors Association of America
5410 Grosvenor Lane, Suite 120
Bethesda, MD 20814

NATIONAL ASSOCIATION OF PLUMBING HEATING-COOLING CONTRACTORS
P.O. Box 6808
180 South Washington Street
Falls Church, VA 22046

APPLIANCE REPAIRER
Appliance repairers service small appliances such as microwave ovens, toasters, fans, heaters, irons and vacuum cleaners. They disassemble the appliance to remove defective part, using power screwdrivers, soldering iron, and handtools and then reassembles the appliance. Some repair major appliances such as refrigerators, freezers, washers, and dryers. Others may handle power tools such as lawnmowers, drills, and power saws. Some technicians specialize in either gas or electrical appliances while others handle both types.

NATIONAL APPLIANCE SERVICE ASSOCIATION
406 West 34th Street, Suite 628
Kansas City, MO 64111

AUDIO-VIDEO REPAIRER
Installs and repairs audio-video equipment, such as tape recorders, public address systems, slide and motion picture projectors, and record players, using handtools, soldering iron, and special testing equipment. Inspects equipment for defects and repairs or replaces parts. Returns equipment to shop for more complicated repairs.

ELECTRONICS TECHNICIANS ASSOCIATION INTERNATIONAL
825 East Franklin Street
Greencastle, IN 46135

INTERNATIONAL SOCIETY OF CERTIFIED ELECTRONIC TECHNICIANS
2708 West Berry, Suite 8
Ft. Worth, TX 76109

AUTOMOBILE REPAIRER

Repairs and overhauls automobiles, buses, trucks, and other automotive vehicles: Examines vehicle and discusses with customer or Automobile Repair Service Estimator; Automobile Tester; or Bus Inspector nature and extent of damage or malfunction. Plans work procedure, using charts, technical manuals, and experience. Raises vehicle, using hydraulic jack or hoist, to gain access to mechanical units bolted to underside of vehicle. Removes unit, such as engine, transmission, or differential, using wrenches and hoist. Disassembles unit and inspects parts for wear, using micrometers, calipers, and thickness gages. Repairs or replaces parts, such as pistons, rods, gears, valves, and bearings, using mechanic's handtools. Overhauls and replaces carburetors, blowers, generators, distributors, starters, and pumps. Rebuilds parts, such as crankshafts and cylinder blocks, using lathes, shapers, drill presses, and welding equipment. Rewires ignition system, lights, and instrument panel. Relines and adjusts brakes, alines front end, repairs or replaces shock absorbers, and solders leaks in radiator. Mends damaged body and fenders by hammering out or filling in dents and welding broken parts. Replaces and adjusts headlights, and installs and repairs accessories, such as radios, heaters, mirrors, and windshield wipers. May be designated according to specialty as AUTOMOBILE MECHANIC, MOTOR; BUS MECHANIC; DIFFERENTIAL REPAIRER; ENGINE REPAIR MECHANIC, BUS; FOREIGN CAR MECHANIC; TRUCK MECHANIC. When working in service station may be designated AUTOMOBILE SERVICE STATION MECHANIC.

AUTOMOTIVE PARTS REBUILDERS ASSOCIATION
6849 Old Dominion Drive, Suite 352
McLean, VA 22101

AUTOMATIC TRANSMISSION REBUILDERS ASSOCIATION
2472 Eastman Avenue, Suite 23
Ventura, CA 93003

AUTOMOTIVE ENGINE REBUILDERS ASSOCIATION
234 Waukegan Road
Glenview, IL 60025

AUTOMOTIVE SERVICE ASSOCIATION
1901 Airport Freeway
P.O. Box 929
Bedford, TX 76021

AUTOMOBILE BODY REPAIRER

Repairs damaged bodies and body parts of automotive vehicles, such as automobiles, buses, and light trucks according to repair manuals, using handtools and power tools: Examines damaged vehicles and estimates cost of repairs. Removes upholstery, accessories, electrical and hydraulic window and seat operating equipment, and trim to gain access to vehicle body and fenders. Positions dolly block against surface of dented area and beats opposite surface to remove dents, using hammer. Fills depressions with solder or other plastic material. Removes damaged fenders, panels, and grills, using wrenches and cutting torch, and bolts or welds replacement parts in position, using wrenches or welding equipment. Straightens bent frames, using hydraulic jack and pulling device. Files, grinds, and sands repaired surfaces, using power tools and handtools. Refinishes repaired surface, using paint spray gun and sander. Aims headlights, alines wheels, and bleeds hydraulic brake system. May paint surfaces after performing body repairs. May repair or replace defective mechanical parts.

AUTOMOTIVE SERVICE INDUSTRY ASSOCIATION
444 North Michigan Avenue
Chicago, IL 60611

NATIONAL INSTITUTE FOR AUTOMOTIVE SERVICE EXCELLENCE
1920 Association Drive, Suite 400
Reston, VA 22091

BICYCLE REPAIRER

Repairs and services bicycles, using power tools and handtools: Tightens and loosens spokes to aline wheels. Disassembles axle to repair coaster brakes and to adjust and replace defective parts, using handtools. Adjusts cables or replaces worn or damaged parts to repair handbrakes. Installs and adjusts speed and gear mechanisms. Shapes replacement parts, using bench grinder. Installs, repairs, and replaces equipment or accessories, such as handle bars, stands, lights, and seats. Paints bicycle frame, using spray gun or brush. Rubs tubes with scraper and places patch over hole to repair tube. May weld broken or cracked frame together, using oxyacetylene torch and welding rods. May assemble and sell new bicycles and accessories.

AMERICAN BICYCLE ASSOCIATION
P.O. Box 718
Chandler, AZ 85244

BICYCLE WHOLESALE DISTRIBUTORS ASSOCIATION
99 West Hawthorne Avenue
Valley Stream, NY 11580

NATIONAL BICYCLE DEALERS ASSOCIATION
129 Cabrillo, Suite 201
Costa Mesa, CA 92627

CAMERA REPAIRER

Repairs and adjusts cameras, using specialized tools and test devices: Disassembles camera, using handtools. Tests and alines diaphragm, lens mounts, and film transport to minimize optical distortion, using precision gages. Adjusts range and view finders, using fixed focusing target. Calibrates operation of shutter, diaphragm, and lens carriers with dial settings, using electronic or stroboscopic timing instruments. Fabricates or modifies parts, using bench lathe, grinder, and drill press.

PHOTOGRAPHIC MANUFACTURERS & DISTRIBUTORS ASSOCIATION
866 United Nations Plaza
New York, NY 10017

PHOTOGRAPHIC SOCIETY OF AMERICA
2005 Walnut Street
Philadelphia, PA 19103

CASH REGISTER REPAIRER

Tests and repairs cash registers, using handtools, power tools, and circuit test meters: Examines mechanical assemblies, such as printing mechanisms, counters, and keyboards, for worn or damaged parts, using precision gages. Replaces defective parts, or reshapes parts on bench lathe or grinder. Tests electrical control units, wiring, and motors, using circuit test equipment. Replaces defective electrical parts, using handtools and welding and soldering equipment. Cleans and oils moving parts. May service adding machines.

INDEPENDENT CASH REGISTER DEALERS ASSOCIATION
711 East Morehead Street
Charlotte, NC 28202

CHIMNEY SWEEPER AND REPAIRER

Cleans soot from and repairs chimneys: Removes pipe connecting furnace to flue, using handtools. Cleans soot from chimney pit, using vacuum cleaner that automatically discharges into receptacle mounted on truck. Cleans connecting pipes with brush, replaces pipe, and seals joints with cement. Closes fireplace openings and other outlets to clean chimney from above. Lowers weighted bag down flue, withdraws bag which expands and scrapes soot from lining of chimney. Empties bag and inspects interior of chimney to insure completion of cleaning process, using reflecting light of mirror. May brush interior of chimney, boilers, and furnaces.

NATIONAL CHIMNEY SWEEP GUILD
18115 Georgia Avenue
P.O. Box 503
Olney, MD 20832

COIN MACHINE REPAIRER

Installs, services, adjusts, and repairs vending, amusement, and other coin operated machines placed in establishments on concession basis: Assembles machines following specifications, using handtools and power tools. Fills machines with ingredients or products and tests ice making, refrigeration, carbonation, evaporation, dispensing, electrical, and coin handling systems. Examines defective machines to determine causes of malfunctions. Adjusts and repairs machines, replacing worn or defective electrical or mechanical parts, using handtools, such as screwdrivers, hammers, and pliers. May collect coins from machine and make settlements with concessionaires. May replenish vending machines with gum, candy, or other articles.

NATIONAL AUTOMATIC MERCHANDIZING ASSOCIATION
20 North Wacker Drive
Chicago, IL 60606

COMMERCIAL AND INDUSTRIAL ELECTRONIC EQUIPMENT REPAIRER

Commercial and industrial electronic equipment repairers, also called industrial electronics technicians, repair electronic equipment used in industrial automated equipment controls, missile control systems, radar systems, medical diagnostic equipment, transmitters, and antennas. Preventive maintenance is a major responsibility of electronics repairers. Equipment is checked, cleaned, and repaired periodically to detect and prevent major malfunctions. Technicians may maintain a log on each piece of equipment to provide a history of performance problems and repairs. Records are usually kept to show the date and condition of the equipment serviced, and to indicate when it is due to be serviced again. Repairers also have to maintain records of repairs, calibration, and tests. When an equipment breakdown does occur, the repairer first determines that it is in the electronic component of the equipment and checks for common causes of trouble such as loose connections or obviously defective components. If routine checks do not locate the trouble, repairers refer to blueprints and manufacturers' specifications that show connections and provide instruction on how to locate problems. When locating the cause of electronic failures, repairers use several kinds of tools including voltmeters, ohmmeters, signal generators, ammeters, and oscilloscopes. They also may run special diagnostic programs that help pinpoint certain malfunctions. To make repairs, they may replace defective components or wiring, or adjust and calibrate equipment.

NATIONAL ELECTRICAL CONTRACTOR'S ASSOCIATION
7315 Wisconsin Avenue
Bethesda, MD 20814

COMPUTER REPAIRER

Installing and keeping the system working is the job of the computer service technician. Technicians service, repair, and adjust the electronic, electrical, and mechanical parts of the computer. They routinely adjust, lubricate, and clean mechanical parts of printers and sorters. Determining what has malfunctioned in the system is often the most difficult part of the job. Computer service technicians use several types of testing equipment to locate the failure, and run diagnostic programs to pinpoint problems. Some of the most modern and sophisticated computers have a self-diagnosing capacity that directs the technician to the exact source of the problem. Computer service technicians also install new equipment. They lay cables, hook up electrical connections between machines, thoroughly test the new equipment, and correct any problems before the customer uses the machine. Some technicians specialize in maintaining a particular brand or type of equipment or system, or in doing a certain type of repair. For example, some technicians are experts in correcting problems caused by errors in the computer's internal programming. Technicians keep a record of preventative maintenance and repairs on each machine they service. In addition, they fill out time and expense reports, keep parts inventories, and order parts. They are employed by manufacturers of the equipment, maintenance service firms, or organizations with large computer installations.

ELECTRONICS TECHNICIANS ASSOCIATION INTERNATIONAL
825 East Franklin Street
Greencastle, IN 46135

INTERNATIONAL SOCIETY OF CERTIFIED ELECTRONIC TECHNICIANS
2708 West Berry, Suite 8
Ft. Worth, TX 76109

NATIONAL COMPUTER SERVICE NETWORK
90 Crossways Park West
Woodbury, NY 11797

NORTH AMERICAN COMPUTER SERVICE ASSOCIATION
506 Georgetown Drive
Casselberry, FL 32707

ELECTRICAL REPAIRER

Repairs, maintains, and installs electrical systems and equipment, such as motors, transformers, wiring, switches, and alarm systems: Locates and determines electrical malfunction, using test instruments, such as ammeter, oscilloscope, and test lamp. Repairs malfunction by such methods as replacing burnt out elements and fuses, by passing or replacing defective wiring, filing switch contact points, and cleaning or rewiring motors, using handtools. Tests electrical equipment, such as generators and heaters, for safety and efficiency, using standard test equipment. Installs fixtures, motors, and other electrical equipment and makes adjustments, using handtools. Inspects circuits and wiring for specified shielding and grounding and repairs or rewires system according to building codes and safety regulations. May replace bearings in electric motors. May repair mechanical, pneumatic, hydraulic, or electronic components of electrical equipment, using standard tools and gages. May plan layout and wire new installations. May be required to hold license. May be designated according to equipment repaired.

ELECTRONICS TECHNICIANS ASSOCIATION INTERNATIONAL
825 East Franklin Street
Greencastle, IN 46135

INTERNATIONAL SOCIETY OF CERTIFIED ELECTRONIC TECHNICIANS
2708 West Berry, Suite 8
Ft. Worth, TX 76109

ELEVATOR REPAIRER

Repairs and maintains elevators, escalators, and dumb waiters to meet safety regulations and building codes, using handtools, power tools, test lamps, ammeters, voltmeters, and other testing devices: Locates and determines causes of trouble in brakes, motors, switches, and signal and control systems, using test lamps, ammeters, and voltmeters. Disassembles defective units and repairs or replaces parts, such as locks, gears, cables, electric wiring, and faulty safety devices, using handtools. Installs push-button controls and other devices to modernize elevators. Lubricates bearings and other parts to minimize friction.

NATIONAL ASSOCIATION OF ELEVATOR CONTRACTORS
2964 Peachtree, NW, Suite 665
Atlanta, GA 30305

FIRE EXTINGUISHER REPAIRER

Repairs and tests fire extinguishers in repair shops and in establishments, such as factories, homes, garages, and office buildings, using handtools and hydrostatic test equipment: Dismantles extinguisher and examines tubings, horns, head gaskets, cutter discs, and other parts for defects. Replaces worn or damaged parts, using handtools. Cleans extinguishers and recharges them with materials, such as soda water and sulfuric acid, carbon tetrachloride, nitrogen, or patented solutions. Tests extinguishers for conformity with legal specifications, using hydrostatic test equipment. May install cabinets and brackets to hold extinguishers. May sell fire extinguishers.

FIRE EQUIPMENT MANUFACTURERS ASSOCIATION
c/o Thomas Associates, Inc.
1230 Keith Building
Cleveland, OH 44115

NATIONAL ASSOCIATION OF FIRE EQUIPMENT DISTRIBUTORS
c/o Smith, Bucklin & Associates, Managers
111 East Wacker Drive
Chicago, IL 60601

UNITED FIRE EQUIPMENT SERVICE ASSOCIATION
c/o Jim Jarzernbowski
International Fire Equipment
22155 West Highway 22
P.O. Box 141
Lake Zurich, IL 60047

FURNACE CLEANER

Cleans fire pots, ducts, vents, registers, air chambers, and filter screens of domestic furnaces: Scrapes soot and ash from fire pot and smoke chambers, using scraper and wire brush. Cleans filter screens, using solvent. Removes dust-clogged air filters and places clean filters into brackets. Brushes and washes dust from air chamber and ducts, using wire or fiber brush. Removes loose soot, ash, and dust, using hand scoop and portable vacuum cleaner. Examines seams of furnace section for defects, such as cracks, and reports defects to customer or furnace repairer. May extract dust from ducts and jackets, using vacuum equipment. May tighten nuts, bolts, and screws on furnace, using handtools.

NATIONAL ASSOCIATION OF PLUMBING HEATING-COOLING CONTRACTORS
P.O. Box 6808
180 South Washington Street
Falls Church, VA 22046

GENERAL MAINTENANCE MECHANICS

Most craft workers specialize in one kind of work; general maintenance mechanics are jacks-of-all-trades. They repair and maintain machines, mechanical equipment, and buildings, and work on plumbing, electrical, and air-conditioning and heating systems. They build partitions, make plaster or dry wall repairs, and fix or paint roofs, windows, doors, floors, woodwork, and other parts of building structures. They also install, maintain, and repair specialized equipment and machinery found in cafeterias, laundries, hospitals, stores, offices, and factories. Typical duties include replacing faulty electrical switches, repairing air-conditioning motors, and installing water lines. Those in small establishments, where they are often the only maintenance worker, do all repairs except for very large or difficult jobs. In larger establishments, their duties may be limited to a few tasks. General maintenance mechanics inspect and diagnose problems and plan how work will be done, often checking blueprints, repair manuals, and parts catalogs. They obtain supplies and repair parts from distributors or storerooms. They use common hand and power tools such as screwdrivers, saws, drills, wrenches, and hammers as well as specialized equipment and electronic test devices. The replace or fix worn or broken parts, where necessary, or make adjustments. They also do routine preventive maintenance to correct defects before equipment breaks down or buildings deteriorate. They may follow a check list, inspecting belts, checking fluid levels, replacing filters, and so forth. Maintenance mechanics also keep records of maintenance and repair work.

BUILDING & SERVICE CONTRACTORS ASSOCIATION
8315 Lee Highway, Suite 301
Fairfax, VA 22031

MECHANICAL CONTRACTORS ASSOCIATION OF AMERICA
5410 Grosvenor Lane, Suite 120
Bethesda, MD 20814

GLASS REPAIRER, AUTOMOBILE

Replaces broken or pitted windshields and window glass in motor vehicles: Removes broken glass by unscrewing frame, using handtools. Cuts flat safety glass according to specified pattern, using glass cutter. Smooths cut edge of glass by holding against abrasive belt. Applies moisture proofing compound along cut edges and installs glass in vehicle. Weatherproofs window or windshield and prevents it from rattling by installing rubber channeling strips around sides of glass. Installs precut replacement glass to replace curved windows. May replace or adjust parts in window raising mechanism.

NATIONAL GLASS ASSOCIATION
8200 Greensboro Drive, Suite 302
McLean, VA 22102

LAUNDRY-MACHINE REPAIRER

Repairs and maintains washers, driers, extractors, condensers, pumps, blowers, presses, and other laundry equipment: Operates, examines, and dismantles equipment to diagnose cause of malfunction. Repairs or replaces parts, using handtools and measuring instruments. Replaces components, such as bearings, motors, and microswitches. Replaces faulty sections of pipe, valves, and fittings, using plumbing tools. Dismantles steam traps and removes sediment. Removes faceplate from equipment to clean out dust and lint. Replaces worn or torn aprons, roll covers, and pads on mangles. Lubricates machines and equipment, using grease gun and oil cans. May order spare parts.

NATIONAL APPLIANCE SERVICE ASSOCIATION
406 West 34th Street, Suite 628
Kansas City, MO 64111

MEDICAL EQUIPMENT REPAIRER

Repairs, calibrates, and maintains medical equipment and instrumentation used in health-care delivery field: Inspects and installs medical and related technical equipment in medical and research facilities for use by physicians, nurses, scientists, or engineers involved in researching, monitoring, diagnosing, and treating physical ailments or dysfunctions. Services various equipment and apparatus, such as patient monitors, electrocardiographs, blood-gas analyzers, X-ray units, defibrillators, electrosurgical units, anesthesia apparatus, pacemakers, bloodpressure transducers, spirometers, sterilizers, diathermy equipment, in-house television systems, patient-care computers, and other related technical paraphernalia. Repairs, calibrates, and maintains equipment, manufacturers' manuals, troubleshooting techniques, and preventive maintenance schedules. Safety-tests medical equipment and health-care facility's structural environment to insure patient and staff safety from electrical or mechanical hazards. Consults with medical or research staff to ascertain that equipment functions properly and safely, utilizing knowledge of electronics, medical terminology, human anatomy and physiology, chemistry, and physics. May demonstrate and explain correct operation of equipment to medical personnel. May modify or develop instruments or devices, under supervision of medical or engineering staff. May work as salesperson or service technician for equipment manufacturers or their sales representatives.

NATIONAL SOCIETY OF BIOMEDICAL EQUIPMENT TECHNICIANS
1901 North Fort Meyer Drive, Suite 602
Arlington, VA 22209

METEOROLOGICAL EQUIPMENT REPAIRER

Installs, maintains, and repairs electronic, mercurial, aneroid, and other types of weather station equipment, using handtools and electronic testing instruments: Tests meteorological instruments for compliance with printed specifications and schematic diagrams, using voltmeters, oscilloscopes, tube testers, and other test instruments. Inspects barometers, thermographs, and hydrographs, including recording mechanisms, and repairs, adjusts, or replaces defective parts. Calibrates graphs and other recording devices. Installs radar and two-way radio systems to detect and communicate weather signals. Adjusts and repairs masts, supporting structures, clearance lights, control panels, control cabling, and wiring, and other electrical and mechanical devices and equipment, using handtools.

AMERICAN METEOROLOGICAL SOCIETY
45 Beacon Street
Boston, MA 02108

MOTORCYCLE REPAIRER

Repairs and overhauls motorcycles, motor scooters, and similar motor vehicles: Listens to engine, examines vehicle's frame, and confers with customer to determine nature and extent of malfunction or damage. Connects test panel to engine and measures generator output, ignition timing, and other engine performance indicators. Dismantles engine and repairs or replaces defective parts, such as magneto, carburetor, and generator. Removes cylinder heads, grinds valves, and scrapes off carbon, and replaces defective valves, pistons, cylinders, and rings, using handtools and power tools. Hammers out dents and bends in frame, welds tears and breaks, and reassembles and reinstalls engine. Readjusts clutch, brakes, and reassembles and reinstalls engine. Repairs or replaces other motorcycle and motor scooter parts, such as spring fork, headlight, horn, handlebar controls, valve release, gear lever, gasoline and oil tanks, starter, brake lever, and muffler.

MOTOR AND EQUIPMENT MANUFACTURERS ASSOCIATION
Technical Training Council
300 Sylvan Avenue
Englewood Cliffs, NJ 07632-0638

SMALL ENGINE SERVICING DEALERS ASSOCIATION
P.O. Box 6312
St. Petersburg, FL 33736

OFFICE MACHINE REPAIRER

Repairs and services office machines, such as adding, photocopying, computers, accounting, calculating machines, and typewriters, using handtools, power tools, micrometers, and welding equipment: Operates machines to test moving parts and to listen to sounds of machines to locate causes of trouble. Disassembles machine and examines parts, such as gears, guides, rollers, and pinions for wear and defects, using micrometers. Repairs, adjusts, or replaces parts, using handtools, power tools, and soldering and welding equipment. Cleans and oils moving parts. May give instructions in operation and care of machines to machine operators.

NATIONAL OFFICE MACHINE SERVICE ASSOCIATION
15544 Minnesota Avenue
Paramount, CA 90723

SAFE AND VAULT REPAIRER

Installs and repairs safes and vault doors in banks and other establishments: Installs vault doors and deposit boxes in banks, according to blueprints. Removes, repairs, adjusts, and reinstalls safes, vault doors, vault compartments, hinges, and other vault and safe equipment, using handtools and other machines, and equipment, such as lathes, drill presses, and welding and acetylene cutting apparatus. Tests and repairs locks and locking devices. Removes interior and exterior finishes and sprays on new finishes.

NATIONAL ASSOCIATION OF PRIVATE SECURITY VAULTS
3562 North Ocean Boulevard
Ft. Lauderdale, FL 33308

SEWING MACHINE REPAIRER

Repairs and adjusts sewing machines in homes and sewing departments of industrial establishments, using handtools: Turns screws and nuts to adjust machine parts. Regulates length of stroke of needle and horizontal movement of feeding mechanism under needle. Dismantles machines and replaces or repairs broken or worn parts, using handtools. Inspects machines, shafts, and belts. Repairs broken transmission belts. Installs attachments on machines. Initiates orders for new machines or parts. May operate machine tools, such as lathes and drill presses, to make new parts.

AMERICAN HOME SEWING ASSOCIATION
1375 Broadway
New York, NY 10018

INDEPENDENT SEWING MACHINE DEALERS ASSOCIATION
P.O. Box 338
Hilliard, OH 43026

SHOE REPAIRER

Repairs or refinishes shoes, following customers specifications, or according to nature of damage, or type of shoe: Positions shoe on last and pulls and cuts off sole or heel with pincers and knife. Starts machine and holds welt against rotating sanding wheel or rubs with sandpaper to bevel and roughen welt for attachment of new sole. Selects blank or cuts sole or heel piece to approximate size from material, using knife. Brushes cement on new sole or heel piece and on shoe welt and shoe heel. Positions sole over shoe welt or heel piece on shoe heel and pounds, using machine or hammer, so piece adheres to shoe; drives nails around sole or heel edge into shoe; or guides shoe and sole under needle of sewing machine to fasten sole to shoe. Trims sole or heel edge to shape of shoe with knife. Holds and turns shoe sole or heel against revolving abrasive wheel to smooth edge and remove excess material. Brushes edge with stain or polish and holds against revolving buffing wheels to polish edge. Nails heel and toe cleats to shoe. Restitches ripped portions or sews patches over holes in shoe uppers by hand or machine. Dampens portion of shoe and inserts and twists adjustable stretcher in shoes or pull portion of moistened shoe back and forth over warm iron to stretch shoe. May build up portions of shoes by nailing, stapling, or stitching additional material to shoe sole to add height or make other specified alterations to orthopedic shoes. May repair belts, luggage, purses, and other products made of materials, such as canvas, leather, and plastic. May quote charges, receive articles, and collect payment for repairs.

SHOE SERVICE INSTITUTE OF AMERICA
1740 East Joppa Road, Suite 1
Baltimore, MD 21234

SMALL ENGINE REPAIRER

Repairs fractional horsepower gasoline engines used to power lawnmowers, garden tractors, boats, motor cycles, and similar machines, using handtools: Locates causes of trouble, dismantles engines, using handtools, and examines part for defects. Replaces or repairs parts, such as rings and bearings, using handtools. Cleans and adjusts carburetor and magneto. Starts repaired engines and listens to sounds to test performance. Replaces engines on machine. May be designated according to type of engine repaired as LAWNMOWER MECHANIC.

SMALL ENGINE SERVICING DEALERS ASSOCIATION
P.O. Box 6312
St. Petersburg, FL 33736

TELEVISION AND RADIO REPAIRER

Repairs and adjusts radios and television receivers, using handtools and electronic testing instruments: Tunes receiver on all channels and observes audio and video characteristics to locate source of trouble. Adjusts controls to obtain desired density, linearity, focus, and size of picture. Examines chassis for defects. Tests voltages and resistances of circuits to isolate defect, following schematic diagram and using voltmeter, oscilloscope, signal generator, and other electronic testing instruments. Tests and changes tubes. Solders loose connections and repairs or replaces defective parts, using handtools and soldering iron. Repairs radios and other audio equipment. May install television sets. May compute charges for labor and materials. May install radios in automobiles.

ELECTRONIC SERVICE DEALERS ASSOCIATION OF ILLINOIS
4621 North Kedzie Avenue
Chicago, IL 60629

NATIONAL ELECTRONICS SALES AND SERVICE DEALERS ASSOCIATION AND THE INTERNA-TIONAL SOCIETY OF CERTIFIED ELECTRONICS TECHNICIANS
2708 West Berry Street
Fort Worth, TX 76109

ELECTRONIC TECHNICIANS ASSOCIATION
604 North Jackson
Greencastle, IN 46135

UPHOLSTERER

Repairs and rebuilds upholstered furniture, using handtools and knowledge of fabrics and upholstery methods: Removes covering webbing, and padding from seat, arms, back, and sides of workpiece, using tack puller, chisel, and mallet. Removes defective springs by cutting cords or wires that hold them in place. Replaces webbing and springs or reties springs. Measures and cuts new covering material. Installs material on inside of arms, back, and seat, and over outside back and arms of wooden frame. Tacks or sews ornamental trim, such as braid and buttons, to cover or frame. May operate sewing machine to seam cushions and join various selections of covering material. May repair wooden frame of workpiece. May refinish wooden surfaces. May upholster cornices. May repair seats, carpets, curtains, and mattresses.

INTERNATIONAL INSTITUTE OF CARPET & UPHOLSTERY CERTIFICATION
2700 Northeast Ancheson, 6-2-A
Vancouver, WA 98661

NATIONAL ASSOCIATION OF PROFESSIONAL UPHOLSTERERS
P.O. Box 2754
200 South Main
High Point, NC 27261

NATIONAL UNFINISHED FURNITURE INSTITUTE
1850 Oak Street
Northfield, IL 60093

VACUUM CLEANER REPAIRER

Repairs and adjusts vacuum cleaners, using handtools: Observes ammeter reading and listens to sound of cleaner motor to detect cause of faulty operation. Repairs, adjusts, or replaces defective brushes, belts, fans, control switches, extension cords, electric motors, or other mechanical or electrical parts, using handtools. Lubricates cleaner parts, using grease gun. May sell and demonstrate vacuum cleaners.

ASSOCIATION OF VACUUM EQUIPMENT MANUFACTURING
230 North Michigan Avenue, Room 1200
Chicago, IL 60601

VACUUM DEALERS TRADE ASSOCIATION
1200 Locust
Des Moines, IA 50309

SALES

SALES REPRESENTATIVE, AUTOMOTIVE PARTS

Sells spare and replaceable parts and equipment from behind counter in agency, repair shop, or parts store: Ascertains make, year, and type of part needed, inspects damaged part to determine part required, or advises customer of part needed according to description of malfunction. Discusses use and features of various parts, based on knowledge of engines, machinery, or equipment. Reads catalog for stock number, price, and replacement parts. Advises customer on substitution or modification of parts when replacement is not available. Examines returned part to determine if it is defective and exchanges part or refunds money. Fills customer orders from stock, finding parts by location and stock number from catalog. Marks and stores parts in stockroom according to prearranged plan. Receives and fills telephone orders for parts. May measure engine parts to determine whether similar parts may be machined down or built up to required size, using micrometers and knowledge of part specifications, machining, metalizing, and rebuilding operations.

AUTOMOTIVE PARTS & ACCESSORIES ASSOCIATION
5100 Forbes Boulevard
Lanham, MD 20706

AUTOMOTIVE WAREHOUSE DISTRIBUTORS ASSOCIATION
9140 Ward Parkway
Kansas City, MO 64114

NATIONAL AUTOMOTIVE PARTS ASSOCIATION
2999 Circle 75 Parkway
Atlanta, GA 30339

SALES REPRESENTATIVE, BARBER AND BEAUTY EQUIPMENT AND SUPPLIES

Sells barber and beauty equipment and supplies, such as hydraulic chairs, counters, mirrors, hair driers, clippers, brushes, combs, cosmetics, hairdressings, and shampoos, to barber and beauty shops: Advises customers on layout of shop fixtures and equipment.

BEAUTY & BARBER SUPPLY INSTITUTE
155 North Dean Street
Englewood, NJ 07631

BEAUTY SUPPLY CENTER AMERICAN HEALTH & BEAUTY AIDS INSTITUTE
111 East Wacker Drive, Suite 600
Chicago, IL 60601

INDEPENDENT COSMETIC MANUFACTURERS & DISTRIBUTORS
Box 727
Bensenville, IL 60106

SALES REPRESENTATIVE, BURIAL NEEDS

Sells burial needs, such as cemetery plots and crypts, grave coverings, markers, and mausoleums: Contacts prospects at their homes in response to telephone inquiries, referrals from funeral homes, and leads from obituary notices. May sell monuments and similar memorials, either in employ of cemetery or monument firm. May specialize in one type of burial need and be designated accordingly as SALESPERSON, BURIAL PLOTS; SALESPERSON, GRAVE COVERINGS AND MARKERS.

AMERICAN CEMETERY ASSOCIATION
Three Skyline Place, Suite 1111
5201 Leesburg Pike
Falls Church, VA 22041

CREMATION ASSOCIATION OF NORTH AMERICA
111 East Wacker Drive, Suite 600
Chicago, IL 60601

INTERNATIONAL CEMETERY SUPPLY ASSOCIATION
P.O. Box 07779
Columbus, OH 43207

MONUMENT BUILDERS OF NORTH AMERICA
1612 Central Street
Evanston, IL 60201

SALES REPRESENTATIVE, COSMETICS AND TOILETRIES

Sells cosmetics and toiletries, such as skin creams, hair preparations, face powder, lipstick, and perfume, to customers in department store or specialty shop: Demonstrates methods of application of various preparations to customer. Explains beneficial properties of preparations and suggests shades or varieties of makeup to suit customer's complexion. May weigh and mix facial powders, according to established formula, to obtain desired shade, using spatula and scale.

INDEPENDENT COSMETIC MANUFACTURERS & DISTRIBUTORS
Box 727
Bensenville, IL 60106

SALES REPRESENTATIVE, DENTAL AND MEDICAL EQUIPMENT AND SUPPLIES

Sells medical and dental equipment and supplies, except drugs and medicines, to doctors, dentists, hospitals, medical schools, and retail establishments: Studies data describing new products to develop sales approach. Compiles data on equipment and supplies preferred by customers. Advises customers of equipment for given need based on technical knowledge of products. Provides customers with advice in such areas as office layout, legal and insurance regulations, cost analysis, and collection methods to develop goodwill and promote sales. May be designated according to type of equipment and supplies sold as SALES REPRESENTATIVE, DENTAL EQUIPMENT AND SUPPLIES. May sell orthopedic appliances, trusses, and artificial limbs and be designated SALES REPRESENTATIVE, PROSTHETIC AND ORTHOTIC APPLIANCES. May sell services of dental laboratory and be designated as SALES REPRESENTATIVE, DENTAL PROSTHETICS.

ACADEMY OF DENTAL MATERIALS
311 East Chicago Avenue
Chicago, IL 60601

AMERICAN DENTAL TRADE ASSOCIATION
4222 King Street
Alexandria, VA 22302

ASSOCIATION FOR THE ADVANCEMENT OF MEDICAL INSTRUMENTATION
1901 North Fort Myer Drive, Suite 602
Arlington, VA 22209

ASSOCIATION OF TONGUE DEPRESSORS
c/o Matthew Schorr
6940 Town Harbor Boulevard, #2413
Boca Raton, FL 33433

BIOMEDICAL MARKETING ASSOCIATION
505 East Howley Street
Mundelein, IL 60060

DENTAL DEALERS OF AMERICA
1118 Land Title Building
Philadelphia, PA 19110

DENTAL MANUFACTURERS OF AMERICA
1118 Land Title Building
Broad & Chestnut Streets
Philadelphia, PA 19110

HEALTH INDUSTRY DISTRIBUTORS ASSOCIATION
111 East Wacker Drive, Suite 600
Chicago, IL 60601

HEALTH INDUSTRY MANUFACTURERS ASSOCIATION
1030 15th Street, NW, Suite 1100
Washington, DC 200005

INDEPENDENT MEDICAL DISTRIBUTORS ASSOCIATION
5845 Horton, Suite 201
Mission, KS 66209

INTERNATIONAL OXYGEN MANUFACTURERS ASSOCIATION
P.O. Box 16248
Cleveland, OH 44116

NATIONAL HEARING AID SOCIETY
20361 Middlebelt Road
Livonia, MI 48152

ORTHOPEDICS SURGICAL MANUFACTURERS ASSOCIATION
c/o Richards Medical Company
1450 Brooks Road
Memphis, TN 38116

SALES REPRESENTATIVE, HEARING AIDS

Sells hearing aids to customers in retail establishment: Tests customer's hearing, using audiometer, to determine need for hearing aid in cases where customer is not referred to store by PHYSICIAN. Confers with customer concerning particular hearing needs to select type and style of aid. Demonstrates use of aid to customer and fits aid. May replace defective parts or make repairs to equipment returned by customer.

HEARING INDUSTRIES ASSOCIATION
1800 M Street, NW
Washington, DC 20036

NATIONAL HEARING AID SOCIETY
20361 Middlebelt Road
Livonia, MI 48152

SALES REPRESENTATIVE, INSURANCE

Sells insurance to new and present clients, recommending amount and type of coverage based on analysis of prospect's circumstances: Compiles lists of prospective clients to provide leads for additional business. Contacts prospects and explains features and merits of policies offered, utilizing persuasive sales techniques. Calculates and quotes premium rates for recommended policies, using adding machine and rate books. Calls on policyholders to deliver and explain policy, to suggest additions or changes in insurance program, or to make changes in beneficiaries. May collect weekly or monthly premiums from policyholders and keep record of payments. Must have license issued by state. May be designated according to type of insurance sold as SALES AGENT, CASUALTY INSURANCE; SALES AGENT, FIRE INSURANCE; SALES AGENT, LIFE INSURANCE; SALES AGENT, MARINE INSURANCE. May work independently, selling a variety of insurance, such as life, fire, casualty, and marine, for many companies and be designated as INSURANCE BROKER. May work independently, selling for one company, and be designated GENERAL AGENT.

THE COLLEGE OF INSURANCE
101 Murray Street
New York, NY 10007

INDEPENDENT INSURANCE AGENTS OF AMERICA
100 Church Street
New York, NY 10007

NATIONAL ASSOCIATION OF LIFE UNDERWRITERS
1922 F Street, NW
Washington, D.C. 20006

SALES REPRESENTATIVE, MALT LIQUORS
Sells beer and other malt liquors to taverns, hotels, restaurants, cocktail lounges, bowling alleys, steamship companies, railroads, military establishments, delicatessens, and supermarkets for wholesale distributor.

NATIONAL BEER WHOLESALER'S ASSOCIATION
5205 Leesburg Pike, Suite 505
Falls Church, VA 22041

SALES REPRESENTATIVE, ORTHOPEDIC SHOES
Evaluates customer's foot conditions and fits and sells corrective shoes, using knowledge of orthopedics or following prescription: Examines malformed or injured joints and bone structure of customer's feet, or reads PHYSICIAN'S prescription to determine type of corrective shoe required. Selects shoes from stock or draws outline and takes measurements of customer's feet to order custom-

made shoes. Examines shoes on customer's feet to verify correctness of fit.

ORTHOPEDICS SURGICAL MANUFACTURERS ASSOCIATION
c/o Richards Medical Company
1450 Brooks Road
Memphis, TN 38116

SALES REPRESENTATIVE, PHARMACEUTICAL

Promotes use of and sells ethical drugs and other pharmaceutical products to PHYSICIANS, DENTISTS, hospitals, and retail and wholesale drug establishments, utilizing knowledge of medical practices, drugs, and medicines: Calls on customers, informs customer of new drugs, and explains characteristics and clinical studies conducted with drug. Discusses dosage, use, and effect of new drugs, characteristics and medicinal preparations. Gives samples of new drugs to customer. Promotes and sells other drugs and medicines manufactured by company. May sell and take orders for pharmaceutical supply items from persons contacted.

AMERICAN PHARMACEUTICAL ASSOCIATION
2215 Constitution Avenue, NW
Washington, DC 20037

NATIONAL ASSOCIATION OF CHAIN DRUG STORES
P.O. Box 1417-D 49
Alexandria, VA 22313

NATIONAL WHOLESALE DRUGGIST ASSOCIATION
P.O. Box 238
Alexandria, VA 22313

PHARMACEUTICAL MANUFACTURERS ASSOCIATION
1100 15th Street, NW
Washington, DC 20005

SALES REPRESENTATIVE, PUBLIC UTILITIES

Solicits prospective and existing commercial and residential clients to promote increased or economical use of public utilities, such as gas, electric power, telephone, and telegraph service: Inspects installations in existing establishments or reviews plans for new construction to determine potential need or necessity for extension of utility service. Advises customers in most economical use of utility to promote energy conservation and reduce cost. Quotes approximate rates, installation charges, and operating cost and explains company services. Writes construction requisitions and service applications, conforming to needs and requests of consumer. May investigate customers' complaints concerning bills.

May be designated by type of utility sold as SALES REPRESENTATIVE, ELECTRIC SERVICE; SALES REPRESENTATIVE, GAS SERVICE; SALES REPRESENTATIVE, TELEPHONE AND TELEGRAPH SERVICES or by area in which utility is sold as SALES REPRESENTATIVE, RURAL POWER.

UTILITY WORKERS UNION OF AMERICA
815 16th Street, NW
Washington, DC 20006

SALES REPRESENTATIVE, SCHOOL EQUIPMENT AND SUPPLIES
Sells school equipment and supplies, such as blackboards, workbooks, art supplies, science and homemaking equipment, and school furniture.

NATIONAL SCHOOL SUPPLY & EQUIPMENT ASSOCIATION
2020 North 14th Street, Suite 400
Arlington, VA 22201

SALES REPRESENTATIVE, SECURITY SYSTEMS
Sells burglar, fire, and medical emergency alarm systems and security monitoring services to individuals and businesses: Contacts prospective customers to explain security monitoring services and to demonstrate alarm systems. Examines customer's home or business and analyzes customer's requirements to recommend security system to meet customer's needs. Explains operation of security system after installation.

NATIONAL BURGLAR AND FIRE ALARM ASSOCIATION
1120 19th Street, NW, Suite LL-20
Washington, DC 20036

SECURITY EQUIPMENT INDUSTRY ASSOCIATION
2665 30th Street
Santa Monica, CA 90405

SALES REPRESENTATIVE, SURGICAL APPLIANCES
Fits and sells surgical appliances, such as trusses, abdominal supports, braces, cervical collars, and artificial limbs, using knowledge of anatomy, orthopedics, orthotics, and prosthetics: Measures customer with tape measure or follows prescription from PHYSICIAN to determine type and size of appliance required. Selects appliance from stock and fits appliance on customer. Writes specifications for and orders custom-made appliances. May design and fabricate, or direct

fabrication of custom made appliances.

HEALTH INDUSTRY DISTRIBUTORS ASSOCIATION
111 East Wacker Drive, Suite 600
Chicago, IL 60601

NATIONAL ASSOCIATION OF MEDICAL EQUIPMENT SUPPLIERS
618 South Alfred Street
Alexandria, VA 22314

SALES REPRESENTATIVE, USED CARS

Sells used automobiles on premises of automobile agency: Explains features and demonstrates operation of car on lot or on road. Computes and quotes sales price, including tax, trade-in allowance, license fee, and discount, and requirements for financing payment of car on credit.

NATIONAL AUTOMOBILE DEALERS ASSOCIATION
8400 Westpark Drive
McLean, VA 22102

SALES REPRESENTATIVE, VETERINARIAN SUPPLIES

Sells veterinarian and animal hospital instruments, drugs, equipment, supplies, and packaged food.

AMERICAN ANIMAL HOSPITAL ASSOCIATION
Denver West Office Park
P.O. Box 15899
Denver, CO 80215

AMERICAN VETERINARY MEDICAL ASSOCIATION
930 North Meacham Road
Schaumburg, IL 60196

SECURITY AND INVESTIGATION

BODYGUARD

Escorts individuals to protect them from bodily injury, kidnapping, or invasion of privacy. May perform other duties, such as receiving and transcribing dictation or driving motor vehicle to transport individuals to disguise purpose of employment.

GRAPHOLOGIST

Examines handwritten material or other questioned documents to identify author, detect forgery, or determine method used to alter documents: Confers with laboratory specialists, such as chemists and photographers, to determine which scientific processes are necessary to effect analysis. Examines hand or typewritten sample to detect characteristics, such as open loop, quaver, or 't' cross peculiar to an individual, using microscope. Measures angle or slant to estimate degree to which letters and lines vary from perpendicular, using protractor. Compares paper specimen with manufacturer's samples to ascertain type and source. Compares photographic blowup of written or typed specimen obtained from separate sources to ascertain similarity or differences. Works in consultative capacity to various agencies or organizations, including police force, and testifies in legal proceedings.

INVESTIGATOR

Investigates persons or business establishments applying for credit, employment, insurance loans, or settlements of claims: Contacts former employers, neighbors, trade associations, and others by telephone, to verify employment record and to obtain health history and history of moral and social behavior. Examines city directories and public records to verify residence history, convictions and arrests, property ownership, bankruptcies, liens, and unpaid taxes of applicant. Obtains credit rating from banks and credit concerns. Analyzes information gathered by investigation and prepares reports of findings and recommendations. May interview applicant on telephone or in person to obtain other financial and personal data for completeness of report. When specializing in certain types of investigations, may be designated CREDIT REPORTER; INSURANCE-APPLICA-TION INVESTIGATOR.

INVESTIGATOR, FRAUD

Investigates cases of fraud involving use of charge cards reported lost or stolen, cash refunds, and non-existent accounts in retail stores: Receives information from credit, sales, and collection departments regarding suspected fraud cases. Interviews store personnel, and observes and questions suspected customers to obtain evidence. Compiles detailed reports on fraud cases, and submits and discusses cases with police. Consults with postal officials when charge cards are reported stolen in mail. Testifies at court trials of offenders. Prepares reports of fraud cases and submits to security department and other store officials.

INVESTIGATOR, PRIVATE

Conducts private investigations to locate missing persons, obtain confidential information, and solve crimes: Questions individuals to locate missing persons, obtain confidential information, and solve crimes: Questions individuals to locate missing persons. Conducts surveillance of suspects using binoculars and cameras. Conducts background investigation of individual to obtain data on character, financial status, and personal history. Examines scene of crime for clues and submits fingerprints and findings to laboratory for identification and analysis. Writes reports of investigations for clients. Reports criminal information to police and testifies in court. May investigate activities of individuals in divorce and child custody cases. May arrange lie detector tests for employees of clients or witnesses. May escort valuables to protect client's property. May be employed in commercial or industrial establishments for undercover work or be assigned to guard persons.

POLYGRAPH EXAMINER

Interrogates and screens individuals to detect deception or to verify truthfulness, using polygraph equipment and standard polygraph techniques: Attaches apparatus to individual to measure and record changes in respiration, blood pressure, and electrical resistance of skin as result of perspiration changes. Evaluates reactions to questions of a non-emotional nature. Interprets and diagnoses individual's emotional responses to key questions recorded on graph. Visits morgues, examines scene of crime, or contacts other sources, when assigned to criminal case, to gather information for use in interrogating suspects, witnesses, and other persons. Appears in court as witness on matters relating to polygraph examinations, according to formalized procedures. Prepares reports and keeps records on polygraph examinations. May instruct classes in polygraph interrogation techniques, methods, and uses. When analyzing voice stress charted on moving tape by needle or recording device for deception or truthfulness verification, may be designated PSYCHOLOGICAL STRESS EVALUATOR.

SECURITY CONSULTANT

Plans, directs, and oversees implementation of comprehensive security systems for protection of individuals and homes, and business, commercial, and industrial organizations, and investigates various crimes against client: Inspects premises to determine security needs. Studies physical conditions, observes activities, and confers with client's staff to obtain data regarding internal operations. Analyzes compiled data and plans and directs installation of electronic security systems, such as closed circuit surveillance, entry controls, burglar alarms, ultrasonic motion detectors, electric eyes, and outdoor perimeter and microwave alarms. Directs installation and checks operation of electronic security equipment. Plans and directs personal security and safety of individual, family, or group for contracted period. Provides bulletproof limousine and bodyguards to ensure client protection during trips and outings. Suggests wearing bulletproof vest when appropriate. Plans and reviews client travel itinerary, mode of transportation, and accommodations. Travels with client and directs security operations. Investigates crimes committed against client, such as fraud, robbery, arson, and patent infringement. Reviews personnel records of client staff and conducts background investigation of selected members to obtain personal histories, character references, and financial status. Conducts or directs surveillance of suspects and premises to apprehend culprits. Notifies client of security weaknesses and implements procedures for handling, storing, safekeeping, and destroying classified materials. Reports criminal information to authorities and testifies in court.

SECURITY GUARD

Guards industrial or commercial property against fire, theft, vandalism, and illegal entry, performing any combination of the following duties: Patrols, periodically, buildings and grounds of industrial plant or commercial establishment, docks, logging camp area, or worksites. Examines doors, windows, and gates to determine that they are secure. Warns violators of rule infractions, such as loitering, smoking, or carrying forbidden articles, and apprehends or expels miscreants. Inspects equipment and machinery to ascertain if tampering has occurred. Watches for and reports irregularities, such as fire hazards, leaking water pipes, and security doors left unlocked. Observes departing personnel to guard against theft of company property. Sounds alarm or calls police or fire department by telephone in case of fire or presence of unauthorized persons. Permits authorized persons to enter property. May register at watch stations to record time of inspection trips. May record data, such as property damage, unusual occurrences, and malfunctioning of machinery or equipment, for use of supervisory staff. May perform janitorial duties and set thermostatic controls to maintain specified temperature in buildings or cold storage rooms. May tend furnace or boiler. May be deputized to arrest trespassers. May regulate vehicle and pedestrian traffic at plant entrance to maintain orderly flow. May patrol site with guard dog on leash. May watch for fires and be designated as FIRE PATROLLER. May be designated according to shift worked as DAY GUARD; area guarded as DOCK GUARD; WAREHOUSE GUARD; or property guarded as POWDER GUARD. May be designated according to establishment guarded as GROUNDS GUARD, ARBORETUM; GUARD, MUSEUM; WATCH GUARD, RACETRACK; or duty station as COIN-VAULT GUARD. May be designated as GUARD, CONVOY when accompanying or leading truck convoy carrying valuable shipments. Additional titles: ARMED GUARD; CAMP GUARD; DECK GUARD; NIGHT GUARD; PARK GUARD.

AMERICAN FEDERATION OF GUARDS
4157 West Fifth Street, No. 220
Los Angeles, CA 90020

AMERICAN ASSOCIATION OF POLICE POLYGRAPHISTS
c/o Holly S. Merrill-Candy
1918 Sleepy Hollow
Pearland, TX 77581

AMERICAN POLYGRAPH ASSOCIATION
Box 8037
Chattanooga, TN 37411

AMERICAN SOCIETY FOR INDUSTRIAL SECURITY
1655 North Ft. Myer Drive, Suite 1200
Arlington, VA 22209

INTERNATIONAL SECURITY MANAGEMENT ASSOCIATION
400 Atlantic Avenue
Boston, MA 02110

AMERICAN SOCIETY FOR INDUSTRIAL SECURITY
1655 North Ft. Myer Drive, Suite 1200
Arlington, VA 22209

COMMITTEE OF NATIONAL SECURITY COMPANIES
2670 Union Avenue, Suite 514
Memphis, TN 38112

COMMUNICATIONS SECURITY ASSOCIATION
655 15th Street, Suite 320
Washington, DC 20005

COMPUTER SECURITY INSTITUTE
43 Boston Post Road
Northboro, MA 01532

COUNCIL OF INTERNATIONAL INVESTIGATORS
P.O. Box 75600
Washington, DC 20013

INTERNATIONAL ASSOCIATION FOR SHOPPING CENTER SECURITY
2830 Clearview Place, NE, Suite 300
Atlanta, GA 30340

INTERNATIONAL ASSOCIATION OF COMPUTER CRIME INVESTIGATORS
c/o Jack Bologna
150 North Main Street
Plymouth, MI 48170

INTERNATIONAL ASSOCIATION OF CREDIT CARD INVESTIGATORS
1620 Grant Avenue
Novato, CA 94947

INTERNATIONAL ASSOCIATION OF PROFESSIONAL SECURITY CONSULTANTS
P.O. Box 93941
Cleveland, OH 44101

INTERNATIONAL ASSOCIATION OF SECURITY SERVICE
P.O. Box 8202
Northfield, IL 60093

INTERNATIONAL GRAPHOANALYSIS SOCIETY
111 North Canal Street
Chicago, IL 60606

INTERNATIONAL SECURITY MANAGEMENT ASSOCIATION
400 Atlantic Avenue
Boston, MA 02110

INTERNATIONAL SOCIETY OF COMPUTER CRIME INVESTIGATORS
P.O. Box 30276
Oakland, CA 94601

NATIONAL ASSOCIATION OF INVESTIGATIVE SPECIALISTS
P.O. Box 33244
Austin, TX 78764

NATIONAL BURGLAR AND FIRE ALARM ASSOCIATION
1120 19th Street, NW, Suite LL-20
Washington, DC 20036

NATIONAL COUNCIL OF INVESTIGATION & SECURITY SERVICES
1133 15th Street, NW, Suite 620
Washington, DC 20005

NATIONAL SOCIETY FOR GRAPHOLOGY
250 West 57th Street, Suite 2032
New York, NY 10107

UNITED STATES PRIVATE SECURITY & DETECTIVE ASSOCIATION
P.O. Box 6303
Corpus Christi, TX 78411

WORLD ASSOCIATION OF DETECTIVES
P.O. Box 11308
Belmont, CA 94002

SEWAGE AND REFUSE

SANITARY LANDFILL OPERATOR

Performs any combination of following duties to dispose of solid waste materials at landfill site: Operates heavy equipment, such as bulldozer, front-end loader, and compactor to excavate landfill site, transport solid waste materials, and to spread and compact layers of waste and earth cover. Directs incoming vehicles to dumping area. Examines cargo to prohibit disposal of caustic waste, according to government regulations. Sprays poisons and other specified chemicals over waste material to control disease carrying pests. Drives truck to distribute oil or water, over landfill to control dust. Weighs vehicles entering and leaving site and collects dumping fees.

NATIONAL SOLID WASTES MANAGEMENT ASSOCIATION
1730 Rhode Island Avenue, NW, Suite 1000
Washington, DC 20036

WASTEWATER TREATMENT PLANT OPERATOR

Operates sewage treatment, sludge processing, and disposal equipment in wastewater treatment plant to control flow and processing of sewage: Monitors control panels and adjusts valves and gates manually or by remote control to regulate flow of sewage. Observes variations in operating conditions and interprets meter and gage readings and tests results to determine load requirements. Starts and stops pumps, engines, and generators to control flow of raw sewage through filtering, settling, aeration, and sludge digestion processes. Maintains log of operations and records meter and gage readings. Gives directions to wastewater treatment plant attendants and sewage disposal workers in performing routine operations and maintenance. May collect sewage sample, using dipper or bottle and conduct laboratory tests, using testing equipment, such as colorimeter. May operate and maintain power generating equipment to provide steam and electricity for plant. May be designated according to specialized activity or stage in processing.

ASSOCIATION OF BOARDS OF CERTIFICATION
P.O. Box 786
Ames, IA 50010

NATIONAL ENVIRONMENTAL TRAINING ASSOCIATION
8687 Via de Ventura, Suite 214
Scottsdale, AZ 85258

WATER POLLUTION CONTROL FEDERATION
601 Wythe Street
Alexandria, VA 22314

TAILORING

ALTERATION TAILOR

Alters clothing to fit individual customers or repairs defective garments. Removes stitches from garment, using ripper or razor blade. Shortens or lengthens sleeves and legs, expands or narrows waist and chest, raises or lowers collar, and inserts or eliminates padding in shoulders while maintaining drape and proportions of garment. Trims excess material, using scissors. Resews garment, using needle and thread or sewing machine. Repairs or replaces defective garment parts, such as pockets, pocket flaps, and coat linings. May fit garments on customer to determine required alterations.

CUSTOM TAILORS AND DESIGNERS ASSOCIATION
17 East 45th Street
New York, NY 10017

UTILITIES

PLANT OPERATORS, POWER DISTRIBUTORS, AND DISPATCHERS

Power plant operators control the machinery that generates electricity. Power distributors and dispatchers oversee the flow of electricity through substations and over a network of transmission and distribution lines to users. Power generating plant operators, also called switchboard operators, and nuclear power operators regulate and monitor boilers, turbines, generators, auxiliary equipment, switching gear, and nuclear reactors used to generate electricity from a central control room. They operate switches to distribute power demands among generators, combine the current from several generators, and regulate the flow of electricity into powerlines. When power needs change, they start or stop generators, and connect or disconnect them from circuits. Operators monitor instruments to see that electricity is flowing through the plant properly and that voltage is maintained. They also keep records of switching operations and loads on generators, lines, transformers, and power levels within reactors, and prepare reports of unusual incidents or malfunctioning equipment during their shift. Power distributors and dispatchers, also called load dispatchers or systems operators, control the flow of electricity through transmission lines to users. They operate current converters, voltage transformers, and circuit breakers. Dispatchers monitor equipment and record readings at a pilot board, which is a map of the transmission system showing the status of transmission circuits and connections with substations and large industrial users. Dispatchers anticipate power needs such as those control room operators to start or stop boilers and generators to bring production in balance with needs. They handle emergencies such as transformer or transmission line failures and route current around affected areas. They also operate and monitor equipment in substations which step up or step down voltage and operate switchboard levers to control the flow of electricity in and out of substations.

UTILITY WORKERS UNION OF AMERICA
815 16th Street, NW
Washington, DC 20006

VETERINARY

VETERINARIANS

Veterinarians care for pets and livestock, treat sporting animals, and protect the public from exposure to animal diseases. Many enter the field because they like working with animals. Typically, veterinarians diagnose medical problems in their animal patients, perform surgery, and prescribe and administer medicines and drugs. Most veterinarians engage in private practice and treat small companion animals such as dogs, cats, and birds. Many veterinarians concentrate on larger food animals or have a mixed practice of both large and small animals. Companion animal medicine encompasses the prevention, diagnosis, and treatment of pet diseases-typically found in dogs and cats. Veterinarians in this field provide these services in animal hospitals or clinics. Food animal veterinarians specialize in the health care needs of cattle, poultry, swine, fish, and sheep. They provide preventative care by advising ranchers and farmers on the proper care and management of livestock. The type of practice varies by geographic region. Veterinarians in rural areas are more likely to work with livestock and horses than those in metropolitan centers. Since pets are found everywhere, very few veterinarians work exclusively with large animals. A number of veterinarians engage in research, food safety inspection, or education. It is not generally understood that veterinarians contribute to human as well as animal health care. Veterinarians may join physicians and scientists in carrying out research at an academic medical center, for example, and explore such topics as techniques of organ transplantation or the efficacy of a new drug. Some veterinarians are in regulatory medicine or public health. They inspect food, investigate outbreaks of disease, and work in scientific laboratories. Veterinarians help prevent the outbreak and spread of animal diseases, like rabies, that can be transmitted to human beings. A small but significant number of veterinarians specialize in toxicology or animal pathology. Although there have been impressive successes in controlling diseases transmitted through food animals, changing technology and more complex methods of food production present new threats to food safety. Residues from herbicides, pesticides, and antibiotics used in food production pose a particular problem. Scientific advances in livestock production have, paradoxically, created a need for veterinarians capable of dealing with contamination of the food chain by toxic chemicals. Some veterinarians teach in veterinary colleges, work in zoos or animal laboratories, or engage in a combination of clinical and research activities.

AMERICAN ANIMAL HOSPITAL ASSOCIATION
Denver West Office Park
P.O. Box 15899
Denver, CO 80215

AMERICAN VETERINARY MEDICAL ASSOCIATION
930 North Meacham Road
Schaumburg, IL 60196

WRITING AND EDITING

*Warning! Stay within the **industries** of this book. For example, radio and television, writers and editors.*

EDITOR

Formulates policy; plans, coordinates, and directs editorial activities; and supervises workers who assist in selecting and preparing material for publication in books, magazines, trade journals, newspapers, newsletters, radio and television broadcasts, advertisements, and related publications: Confers with executives, department heads, and editorial staff to formulate policy, coordinate department activities, establish production schedules, solve publication problems, and discuss makeup plans and organizational changes. Determines theme of issue and gathers related material. Writes or assigns staff members or free-lance writers to write articles, reports, editorials, reviews, and other material. Reads and evaluates material submitted for publication consideration. Reviews draft of manuscript and makes recommendations for changes. May edit and correct final draft to prepare for typesetting. May select or recommend graphics, such as drawings, diagrams, pictures, and charts to illustrate manuscript. Assigns staff member, or personally interviews individuals and attends gatherings, to obtain items for publication, verify facts, and clarify information. Organizes material, plans overall and individual page layouts, and selects type. Marks dummy pages to indicate position and size of printed and graphic material. Reviews final proofs and approves or makes changes. May direct activities of production, circulation, or promotion personnel. May prepare news or public relations releases, special brochures, and similar materials. May specialize in particular type of publication, such as manuals, books, articles, or proposals.

EDITOR, BOOK

Secures, selects, and coordinates publication of manuscripts in book form: Reviews submitted manuscript, determines demand based on consumer trends and personal knowledge, and makes recommendations regarding procurement and revision. Confers with author and publisher to arrange purchase and details, such as publication date, royalties, and number of copies to be printed. Coordinates design and production activities. May assign and supervise editorial staff. May contract design and production or personally design and produce book.

EDITOR, COPY

Prepares written material for publication, performing any combination of following duties: Reads copy to detect errors in spelling, punctuation, and syntax.

Verifies facts, dates, and statistics, using standard reference sources. Rewrites or modifies copy to conform to publication's style and editorial policy and marks copy for typesetter, using standard symbols to indicate how type should be set. Reads galley and page proofs to detect errors and indicates corrections, using standard proofreading symbols. May confer with authors regarding changes made to manuscript.

EDITOR, DICTIONARY

Researches information about words that make up language and writes and reviews definitions for publication in dictionary: Conducts or directs research to discover origin, spelling, syllabication, pronunciation, meaning, and usage of words. Organizes research material and writes dictionary definition. May study or conduct surveys to determine factors, such as frequency of use for a specific word, or word use by particular segment of population in order to select words for inclusion in dictionary. May perform related editorial duties. May select drawings or other graphic material to illustrate word meaning. May specialize in particular type of dictionary, such as medical, electronic, or industrial.

EDITOR, INDEX

Prepares indexes for books and other publications: Reads material to determine which items should be in index. Arranges topical or alphabetical list of index items, according to page or chapter, indicating location of item in text. Classifies items of topical interest, and inserts cross references in index to refer reader to related subjects appearing elsewhere in text. Directs activities of clerical staff engaged in typing indexes, filing subject-cards, and performing related duties. May prepare related items, such as glossaries, bibliographies, and explanatory footnotes, following literary style of manuscript author.

WRITER

Writers communicate through the written word by developing original fiction and nonfiction prose for books, magazine, trade journals, newspapers, technical studies, reports, newsletters, radio and television broadcasts, and advertisements. Writers gather information on topics through personal observation, research, and interviews. From the information gathered, they select and organize the material to be used, and finally put it into words that will convey it to the reader with the desired effect. Writers often revise or rewrite sections, searching for the best organization of the material or the right phrasing. Newswriters–writers employed by newspapers and radio and television news departments–write news items for inclusion in newspapers or news broadcasts. Technical writers put scientific and technical information into readily understandable language. They prepare manuals, catalogs, parts lists, and instructional materials used by sales representatives to sell a wide variety of machinery and equipment and by technicians to install, maintain, and service it. Copy writers write advertising copy for use by publication or broadcast media to promote the sale of goods and services. Established writers may work on a free-lance basis where they sell their work to publishers or publication units, manufacturing firms, and public relations and advertising departments or agencies.

AMERICAN BOOK SELLERS ASSOCIATION
122 East 42d Street
New York, NY 10168

AMERICAN SOCIETY OF JOURNALISTS & AUTHORS
1501 Broadway, Suite 1907
New York, NY 10036

ASSOCIATION OF EDITORIAL BUSINESSES
116 Fourth Street, NW
Washington, DC 20003

AUTHORS LEAGUE OF AMERICA
234 West 44th Street
New York, NY 10036

COMMITTEE OF SMALL MAGAZINE EDITORS & PUBLISHERS
P.O. Box 703
San Francisco, CA 94101

EDITORIAL FREE-LANCERS ASSOCIATION
P.O. Box 2050
Madison Square Station
New York, NY 10159

NATIONAL WRITERS CLUB
1450 South Havana, Suite 620
Aurora, CO 80012

Recession- and Depressionproof

BUSINESSES

AMBULANCE

AIR LIFELINE
1011 St. Andrews Drive, Suite I
El Dorado Hills, CA 95630

AMERICAN AMBULANCE ASSOCIATION
3814 Auburn Boulevard, Suite 70
Sacramento, CA 95821

ARMORED CAR

ARMORED TRANSPORTATION INSTITUTE
P.O. Box 333
Baltimore, MD 21203

NATIONAL ARMORED CAR ASSOCIATION
P.O. Box 19745
Seattle, WA 98109

AUTOMOBILE SALVAGE

AUTOMOTIVE DISMANTLERS & RECYCLERS ASSOCIATION
1133 15th Street, NW
Washington, DC 20005

INSTITUTE OF SCRAP RECYCLING INDUSTRIES
1627 K Street, NW, Suite 700
Washington, DC 20006

AUTOMOBILE SUPPLY STORE

AUTOMOTIVE PARTS & ACCESSORIES ASSOCIATION
5100 Forbes Boulevard
Lanham, MD 20706

AUTOMOTIVE WAREHOUSE DISTRIBUTORS ASSOCIATION
9140 Ward Parkway
Kansas City, MO 64114

AUTOMOBILE TOWING

INTERSTATE TOWING ASSOCIATION
615 East Eighth Street
P.O. Box 801
Traverse City, MI 49685

AUTOMOTIVE PARTS REBUILDING

AUTOMATIC TRANSMISSION REBUILDERS ASSOCIATION
2472 Eastman Avenue, Suite 23
Ventura, CA 93003

AUTOMOTIVE ENGINE REBUILDERS ASSOCIATION
234 Waukegan Road
Glenview, IL 60025

AUTOMOTIVE PARTS REBUILDERS ASSOCIATION
6849 Old Dominion Drive, Suite 352
McLean, VA 22101

BARBER AND BEAUTY SUPPLY

BEAUTY & BARBER SUPPLY INSTITUTE
155 North Dean Street
Englewood, NJ 07631

BEAUTY SUPPLY CENTER AMERICAN HEALTH & BEAUTY AIDS INSTITUTE
111 East Wacker Drive, Suite 600
Chicago, IL 60601

INDEPENDENT COSMETIC MANUFACTURERS & DISTRIBUTORS
Box 727
Bensenville, IL 60106

CLEANING

BUILDING SERVICE CONTRACTORS ASSOCIATION INTERNATIONAL
8315 Lee Highway, Suite 301
Fairfax, VA 22031

CLEANING & MANAGEMENT INSTITUTE
17911-C Skypark Boulevard
Irvine, CA 92714

COIN OPERATED LAUNDRY

COIN LAUNDRY ASSOCIATION
1315 Butterfield Road, Suite 212
Downers Grove, IL 60515

CREDIT REPORTING AND COLLECTION

AMERICAN COLLECTORS ASSOCIATION, INC.
4040 West 70th Street
P.O. Box 35106
Minneapolis, MN 55435

AMERICAN RECOVERY ASSOCIATION
P.O. Box 6788
New Orleans, LA 70174

ASSOCIATED CREDIT BUREAUS
16211 Park Ten Place
P.O. Box 218300
Houston, TX 77218

INTERNATIONAL ASSOCIATION OF CREDIT CARD INVESTIGATORS
1620 Grant Avenue
Novato, CA 94947

INTERNATIONAL CREDIT ASSOCIATION
2243 North Lindbergh
P.O. Box 27357
St. Louis, MO 63141

NATIONAL ASSOCIATION OF CREDIT MANAGEMENT
520 Eighth Avenue
New York, NY 10018

DRY CLEANING

INSTITUTE OF INDUSTRIAL LAUNDERERS
1730 M Street, NW, Suite 610
Washington, DC 20036

INTERNATIONAL FABRICARE INSTITUTE
12251 Tech Road
Silver Springs, MD 20904

INTERNATIONAL DRY-CLEANERS CONGRESS
P.O. Box 8629
San Jose, CA 95155

NATIONAL ASSOCIATION OF INSTITUTIONAL LINEN MANAGEMENT
2130 Lexington Road, Suite H
Richmond, KY 40475

TEXTILE CARE ALLIED TRADES ASSOCIATION
543 Valley Road
Upper Montclair, NJ 07043

EMPLOYMENT AGENCY

ASSOCIATION OF EXECUTIVE SEARCH CONSULTANTS
151 Railroad Avenue
Greenwich, CT 06830

EMPLOYMENT MANAGEMENT ASSOCIATION
20 William Street
Wellesley, MA 02181

NATIONAL ASSOCIATION OF PERSONNEL CONSULTANTS
1432 Duke Street
Alexandria, VA 22314

NATIONAL ASSOCIATION OF TEMPORARY SERVICES
119 South Asaph Street
Alexandria, VA 22314

NATIONAL PERSONNEL CONSULTANTS
535 Court Street
P.O. Box 1379
Reading, PA 19603

FIRE FIGHTING EQUIPMENT AND SUPPLIES

FIRE EQUIPMENT MANUFACTURERS ASSOCIATION
c/o Thomas Associates, Inc.
1230 Keith Building
Cleveland, OH 44115

NATIONAL ASSOCIATION OF FIRE EQUIPMENT DISTRIBUTORS
c/o Smith, Bucklin & Associates, Managers
111 East Wacker Drive
Chicago, IL 60601

UNITED FIRE EQUIPMENT SERVICE ASSOCIATION
c/o Jim Jarzernbowski
International Fire Equipment
22155 West Highway 22
P.O. Box 141
Lake Zurich, IL 60047

FLEA MARKETS

CLARK'S FLEA MARKET U.S.A
Clark's Publications
2156 Cotton Patch Lane
Milton, FL 32570

FUNERAL SERVICE, EQUIPMENT, AND SUPPLIES

AMERICAN BOARD OF FUNERAL SERVICE EDUCATION
P.O. Box 2098
201 Columbia Street
Fairmont, WV 22655

AMERICAN CEMETERY ASSOCIATION
Three Skyline Place, Suite 1111
5201 Leesburg Pike
Falls Church, VA 22041

ASSOCIATED FUNERAL DIRECTORS SERVICE INTERNATIONAL
P.O. Box 7476
810 Stratford Avenue
Tampa, FL 33603

CASKET MANUFACTURERS ASSOCIATION OF AMERICA
708 Church Street
Evanston, IL 60201

CREMATION ASSOCIATION OF NORTH AMERICA
111 East Wacker Drive, Suite 600
Chicago, IL 60601

EMBALMING CHEMICAL MANUFACTURERS ASSOCIATION
c/o R. Beck
Embalmers Supply Co
P.O. Box 631
Westport, CT 06881

INTERNATIONAL CEMETERY SUPPLY ASSOCIATION
P.O. Box 07779
Columbus, OH 43207

MONUMENT BUILDERS OF NORTH AMERICA
1612 Central Street
Evanston, IL 60201

NATIONAL CONCRETE BURIAL VAULT ASSOCIATION
P.O. Box 1031
Battle Creek, MI 49016

NATIONAL FUNERAL DIRECTORS ASSOCIATION
135 West Wells Street, Suite 600
Milwaukee, WI 53203

NATIONAL FUNERAL DIRECTORS & MORTICIANS ASSOCIATION
5723 South Indiana Avenue
Chicago, IL 60637

NATIONAL SELECTED MORTICIANS
1616 Central Street
Evanston, IL 60210

TELOPHASE SOCIETY (MORTUARY SERVICES & BURIAL AT SEA)
1333 Camino Del Rio South
San Diego, CA 92108

FURNITURE RENTING AND LEASING

FURNITURE RENTAL ASSOCIATION OF AMERICA
5008 Pine Creek Drive, Suite B
Westerville, OH 43081

HOME HEALTH CARE

AMERICAN ASSOCIATION FOR CONTINUITY OF CARE
1101 Connecticut Avenue, NW, Suite 700
Washington, DC 20036

AMERICAN FEDERATION OF HOME HEALTH AGENCIES
1320 Fenwick Lane, Suite 500
Silver Spring, MD 20910

FOUNDATION FOR HOSPICE & HOME CARE
519 C Street, NE
Stanton Park
Washington, DC 20002

NATIONAL ASSOCIATION FOR HOME CARE
519 C Street, NE
Stanton Park
Washington, DC 20002

LIQUOR STORE

AMERICAN BEVERAGE ALCOHOL ASSOCIATION
Ten East 40th Street, Room 2000
New York, NY 10016

NATIONAL LIQUOR STORE ASSOCIATION
5101 River Road, Suite 108
Bethesda, MD 20816

MEDICAL AND DENTAL EQUIPMENT AND SUPPLIES

ACADEMY OF DENTAL MATERIALS
311 East Chicago Avenue
Chicago, IL 60601

AMERICAN ORTHOTIC & PROSTHETIC ASSOCIATION
717 Pendleton Street
Alexandria, VA 22314

ASSOCIATION FOR THE ADVANCEMENT OF MEDICAL INSTRUMENTATION
1901 North Fort Myer Drive, Suite 602
Arlington, VA 22209

ASSOCIATION OF TONGUE DEPRESSORS
c/o Matthew Schorr
6940 Town Harbor Boulevard, #2413
Boca Raton, FL 33433

BIOMEDICAL MARKETING ASSOCIATION
505 East Howley Street
Mundelein, IL 60060

DENTAL DEALERS OF AMERICA
1118 Land Title Building
Philadelphia, PA 19110

DENTAL MANUFACTURERS OF AMERICA
1118 Land Title Building
Broad and Chestnut Streets
Philadelphia, PA 19110

HEALTH INDUSTRY DISTRIBUTORS ASSOCIATION
111 East Wacker Drive, Suite 600
Chicago, IL 60601

HEALTH INDUSTRY MANUFACTURERS ASSOCIATION
1030 15th Street, NW, Suite 1100
Washington, DC 20005

INDEPENDENT MEDICAL DISTRIBUTORS ASSOCIATION
5845 Horton, Suite 201
Mission, KS 66209

INTERNATIONAL OXYGEN MANUFACTURERS ASSOCIATION
P.O. Box 16248
Cleveland, OH 44116

NATIONAL ASSOCIATION OF MEDICAL EQUIPMENT SUPPLIERS
618 South Alfred Street
Alexandria, VA 22314

NATIONAL HEARING AID SOCIETY
20361 Middlebelt Road
Livonia, MI 48152

ORTHOPEDICS SURGICAL MANUFACTURERS ASSOCIATION
c/o Richards Medical Company
1450 Brooks Road
Memphis, TN 38116

MEDICAL LABORATORY SERVICE

AMERICAN ASSOCIATION OF BIOANALYSTS
818 Olive Street, Suite 918
St. Louis, MO 63101

AMERICAN CLINICAL LABORATORY ASSOCIATION
1919 Pennsylvania Avenue, NW, Suite 800
Washington, DC 20006

INTERNATIONAL SOCIETY FOR CLINICAL LABORATORY TECHNOLOGY
818 Olive Street, Suite 918
St. Louis, MO 63101

NATIONAL CERTIFICATION FOR MEDICAL LABORATORY PERSONNEL
1725 De Sales Street, NW, Suite 403
Washington, DC 20036

NATIONAL COMMITTEE FOR CLINICAL LABORATORY STANDARDS
771 East Lancaster Avenue
Villanova, PA 19085

MOVING SERVICE, RESIDENTIAL

AMERICAN MOVERS CONFERENCE
2200 Mill Road
Alexandria, VA 22314

MOVERS & WAREHOUSEMEN'S ASSOCIATION OF AMERICA
1001 North Highland Street
Arlington, VA 22201

NATIONAL INSTITUTE OF MOVING CONSULTANTS
124 South Royal Street
Alexandria, VA 22314

NATIONAL MOVING & STORAGE ASSOCIATION
124 South Royal Street
Alexandria, VA 22314

NEWSPAPER

AMERICAN NEWSPAPER PUBLISHERS ASSOCIATION
Newspaper Center
Box 17407
Dulles International Airport
Washington, DC 20041

NATIONAL NEWSPAPER PUBLISHERS ASSOCIATION
970 National Press Building, Room 948
Washington, DC 20045

NURSING HOME

AMERICAN ASSOCIATION OF HOMES FOR AGING
1129 20th Street, NW, Suite 400
Washington, DC 20036

AMERICAN COLLEGE OF HEALTH CARE ADMINISTRATORS
4650 East - West Highway
P.O. Box 5890
Bethesda, MD 20814

AMERICAN HEALTH CARE ASSOCIATION
1200 15th Street, NW
Washington, DC 20005

NATIONAL GERIATRICS SOCIETY
212 West Wisconsin Avenue, 3rd Floor
Milwaukee, WI 53203

PHARMACY

AMERICAN ASSOCIATION OF COLLEGES OF PHARMACY
4720 Montgomery Lane, Suite 602
Bethesda, MD 20814

AMERICAN FOUNDATION OF PHARMACEUTICAL EDUCATION
Radburn Plaza Building
14-25 Plaza Road
Fairlawn, NJ 07410

AMERICAN PHARMACEUTICAL ASSOCIATION
2215 Constitution Avenue, NW
Washington, DC 20037

AMERICAN SOCIETY OF CONSULTANT PHARMACISTS
2300 Ninth Street, South
Arlington, VA 22204

AMERICAN SOCIETY OF HOSPITAL PHARMACISTS
4630 Montgomery Avenue
Bethesda, MD 20814

ASSOCIATED CHAIN DRUG STORES
212 Fifth Avenue
New York, NY 10010

NATIONAL ASSOCIATION OF RETAIL DRUGGISTS
205 Daingerfield Road
Alexandria, VA 22314

NATIONAL ASSOCIATION OF CHAIN DRUG STORES
P.O. Box 1417-D 49
Alexandria, VA 22313

NATIONAL ASSOCIATION OF MAIL SERVICE PHARMACIES
510 King Street, Suite 420
Alexandria, VA 22314

NATIONAL WHOLESALE DRUGGIST ASSOCIATION
P.O. Box 238
Alexandria, VA 22313

PHARMACEUTICAL MANUFACTURERS ASSOCIATION
1100 15th Street, NW
Washington, DC 20005

PRINTING AND PUBLISHING

*Warning! Stay within the other **industries** of this book. For example, medical publishing.*

AMERICAN BOOK SELLERS ASSOCIATION
122 East 42d Street
New York, NY 10168

ASSOCIATION OF AMERICAN PUBLISHERS
2005 Massachusetts Avenue, NW
Washington, DC 20036

COMMITTEE OF SMALL MAGAZINE EDITORS & PUBLISHERS
P.O. Box 703
San Francisco, CA 94101

PRINTING INDUSTRIES OF AMERICA
1730 North Lynn Street
Arlington, VA 22209

NATIONAL PRINTING EQUIPMENT AND SUPPLY ASSOCIATION
1899 Preston White Drive
Reston, VA 22091

RECYCLING

ALUMINUM RECYCLING ASSOCIATION
1000 16th Street, NW
Washington, DC 20036

AUTOMOTIVE DISMANTLERS & RECYCLERS ASSOCIATION
1133 15th Street, NW
Washington, DC 20005

INSTITUTE OF SCRAP RECYCLING INDUSTRIES
1627 K Street, NW, Suite 700
Washington, DC 20006

NATIONAL RECYCLING COALITION
P.O. Box 80729
Lincoln, NE 68501

STEEL CAN RECYCLING ASSOCIATION
Two Gateway Center, Suite 720
Pittsburgh, PA 15222

RENTAL

(tools, medical equipment, machinery, moving trucks and trailers, etc.)

AMERICAN RENTAL ASSOCIATION
1900 19th Street
Moline, IL 61265

SCHOOL SUPPLIES

NATIONAL SCHOOL SUPPLY & EQUIPMENT ASSOCIATION
2020 North 14th Street, Suite 400
Arlington, VA 22201

SECOND HAND AND SURPLUS STORES

ASSOCIATED SURPLUS DEALERS
P.O. Box 250046
Los Angeles, CA 90025

SECURITY EQUIPMENT AND SYSTEMS

NATIONAL ASSOCIATION OF PRIVATE SECURITY VAULTS
135 West Morehead Street
Charlotte, NC 28202

NATIONAL BURGLAR & FIRE ALARM ASSOCIATION
1120 19th Street, NW, Suite LL-20
Washington, DC 20036

SECURITY EQUIPMENT INDUSTRY ASSOCIATION
2665 30th Street
Santa Monica, CA 90405

SEPTIC TANK CLEANING AND REPAIR

AMERICAN SOCIETY OF PLUMBING ENGINEERS
3617 Thousand Oaks Boulevard, Suite 210
West Lake, CA 91362

NATIONAL ASSOCIATION OF PLUMBING-HEATING-COOLING CONTRACTORS
P.O. Box 6808
180 South Washington Street
Falls Church, VA 22046

TRANSPORTATION

AMERICAN BUS ASSOCIATION
1025 Connecticut Avenue, NW
Washington, DC 20036

VETERINARY EQUIPMENT AND SUPPLIES

AMERICAN ANIMAL HOSPITAL ASSOCIATION
Denver West Office Park
P.O. Box 15899
Denver, CO 80215

AMERICAN VETERINARY MEDICAL ASSOCIATION
930 North Meacham Road
Schaumburg, IL 60196

VISION CENTER

AMERICAN ACADEMY OF OPTOMETRY
5530 Wisconsin Avenue, NW, Suite 745
Washington, DC 20815

AMERICAN OPTOMETRIC ASSOCIATION
243 North Lindbergh Boulevard
St. Louis, MO 63141

ASSOCIATION OF SCHOOLS & COLLEGES OF OPTOMETRY
6110 Executive Boulevard, Suite 514
Rockville, MD 20852

CONTACT LENS SOCIETY OF AMERICA
P.O. Box 10115
Fairfax, VA 22030

NATIONAL ASSOCIATION OF MANUAL OPTICIANS
13140 Coit Road, LB 144
Dallas, TX 75240

NATIONAL ASSOCIATION OF OPTOMETRISTS & OPTICIANS
18903 South Miles Road
Cleveland, OH 44128

OPTICIANS ASSOCIATION OF AMERICA
10341 Democracy Lane
P.O. Box 10110
Fairfax, VA 22030

Recession- and Depressionproof

INDUSTRIES

INDUSTRIES

ACCOUNTING AND AUDITING

ARMED FORCES

AUCTIONEERING

CLEANING

CREDIT, COLLECTION, AND REPORTING

DENTAL SERVICES, EQUIPMENT, AND SUPPLIES

DIETETICS

EDUCATION

FIREFIGHTING, EQUIPMENT, AND SUPPLIES

FUNERAL SERVICES, EQUIPMENT, AND SUPPLIES

HAIRSTYLING

INSURANCE

LAW AND JURISPRUDENCE

LAW ENFORCEMENT

LOCKS AND LOCKSMITHING

MEDICAL SERVICES, EQUIPMENT, AND SUPPLIES

NEWSPAPER PUBLISHING

PERSONNEL SERVICES

PEST CONTROL

PHARMACEUTICAL

PRINTING AND PUBLISHING

RADIO AND TELEVISION

RELIGION

REPAIR AND MAINTENANCE

SECURITY AND INVESTIGATION

SEWAGE AND REFUSE

UTILITIES

VETERINARY

WRITING AND EDITING

RECESSION- AND DEPRESSIONPROOF OCCUPATIONS YOU CAN LEARN IN TWO YEARS OR LESS

OCCUPATIONS	WEEKS
AIR CONDITIONING/REFRIGERATION TECHNICIAN	12-73
APPLIANCE REPAIRER	12-72
ARTIST, COMMERCIAL	52-136
AUTOMOBILE BODY REPAIRER	26-52
AUTOMOTIVE MECHANIC	14-50
BARBER/HAIRSTYLIST	32-52
BROADCAST TECHNICIAN	10-92
BROADCASTER	13-48
BUILDING MAINTENANCE TECHNICIAN	52-60
CAMERA REPAIRER	16-50
COIN-OPERATED MACHINE REPAIRER	26
COMPUTER REPAIRER	30-120
COSMETOLOGIST	52
COURT REPORTER	104
DENTAL ASSISTANT	12-50
DENTAL LABORATORY TECHNICIAN	26-72
DIETETIC TECHNICIAN	13-52
EMERGENCY MEDICAL TECHNICIAN	28-34
HEATING MECHANIC	12-24
LEGAL ASSISTANT/PARALEGAL	24-52
LEGAL SECRETARY	16-72
LOCKSMITH	10
LOSS PREVENTION/SECURITY OFFICER	16
MEDICAL ASSISTANT	12-48
MEDICAL/DENTAL RECEPTIONIST	16-27
MEDICAL LAB TECHNICIAN	48-72
MEDICAL OFFICE MANAGER	14-28
MEDICAL SECRETARY	52
MOTORCYCLE MECHANIC	12-33
NURSE'S AIDE	10-49
OFFICE MACHINE REPAIRER	15-50

OCCUPATIONS	WEEKS
OPERATING ROOM TECHNICIAN	32-42
OPTOMETRIC ASSISTANT	24
PHYSICAL THERAPIST	42
PLUMBER	26
PROPERTY MANAGER	6
SECRETARY/TRANSCRIPTIONIST	24-38
SURGICAL TECHNICIAN	52
UPHOLSTERER	10-26
VOCATIONAL NURSE	48
X-RAY TECHNICIAN	100

SCHOOLS THAT OFFER CORRESPONDENCE COURSES

VOCATIONAL SCHOOLS

NATIONAL HOME STUDY COUNCIL
1601 18th Street, NW, Washington, DC 20009
Offers free information about sources of vocational homestudy programs.

ACADEMIC SCHOOLS

ARIZONA STATE UNIVERSITY
University of Continuing Education, ASB 110, Tempe, AZ 85281

ARKANSAS STATE UNIVERSITY
Center for Continuing Education, Correspondence Department, State University, AR 72467

AUBURN UNIVERSITY
Office of Extended Education and Human Development Services, 3002 Haley Center, Auburn, AL 36830

AZUSA PACIFIC COLLEGE
Universal College Program, Highway 66 at Citrus, Azusa, CA 91702

BALL STATE UNIVERSITY
School of Continuing Education, Muncie, IN 47306

BRIGHAM YOUNG UNIVERSITY
Independent Study, 210 HRCB, Provo, UT 84602

CALIFORNIA STATE UNIVERSITY
Department of Civil Engineering, 6000 J Street, Sacramento, CA 95819

CENTRAL MICHIGAN UNIVERSITY
Office of Independent Study by Correspondence, School of Continuing Education, Mount Pleasant, MI 48859

COLORADO STATE UNIVERSITY
Center for Continuing Education, Rockwell Hall, Fort Collins, CO 80523

EASTERN MICHIGAN UNIVERSITY
Director of Credit Programs, 323 Goodson Hall, Ypsilanti, MI 48197

HOME STUDY INSTITUTE
Tacoma Park, Washington, DC 20012
Offers courses from elementary school through college level.

INDIANA STATE UNIVERSITY
Independent Study, AC220, Terre Haute, IN 47809

INDIANA UNIVERSITY
Independent Study Division, Owen Hall 001, Bloomington, IN 47405

LOUISIANA STATE UNIVERSITY
Correspondence Study Department, Baton Rouge, LA 70803

LOYOLA UNIVERSITY
Correspondence Study Division, 820 North Michigan Avenue, Chicago, IL 60611

MASSACHUSETTS DEPARTMENT OF EDUCATION
Supervisor of Correspondence Instruction, Bureau of Adult Services, 31 St. James Avenue, Boston, MA 02116

MISSISSIPPI STATE UNIVERSITY
Division of Continuing Education, Drawer 5247, Mississippi State, MS 39762

MURRAY STATE UNIVERSITY
Extended Education, Sparks Hall, Murray, KY 42071

NORTH DAKOTA DIVISION OF INDEPENDENT STUDY
Box 5036, State University Station, Fargo, ND 58105

NORTHERN MICHIGAN UNIVERSITY
Off-Campus Education, 410 Cohodas Administrative Center, Marquette, MI 49855

OAKLAND UNIVERSITY
Division of Continuing Education, Rochester, MI 48063
Offers noncredit courses only in management, business, and communication.

OHIO UNIVERSITY
Independent Study, Tupper Hall 304, Athens, OH 45701

OKLAHOMA STATE UNIVERSITY
Independent and Correspondence Study, 018 Classroom Building, Stillwater, OK 74074

OREGON STATE SYSTEM OF HIGHER EDUCATION
Office of Independent Study, Division of Continuing Education, P.O. Box 1491, Portland, OR 97207

PENNSYLVANIA STATE UNIVERSITY
Department of Independent Study by Correspondence, 3 Shields Building, University Park, PA 16802

PURDUE UNIVERSITY
Division of Independent Study, 116 Stewart Center, West Lafayette, IN 47907
Offers only two courses: one in pharmacy, one in pest control.

ROOSEVELT UNIVERSITY
College of Continuing Education, 430 South Michigan Avenue, Chicago, IL 60605

SEMINARY EXTENSION HOME STUDY INSTITUTE
Southern Baptist Convention Building, 460 James Robertson Parkway, Nashville, TN 37219
Offers courses in religion and theology.

TEXAS TECHNICAL UNIVERSITY
Division of Continuing Education, P.O. Box 4110, Lubbock, TX 74909

U.S. DEPARTMENT OF AGRICULTURE GRADUATE SCHOOL
Correspondence Study Programs, Room 6847, South Building, Washington, DC 20250
Designed for government employees but open to all.

UNIVERSITY OF ALABAMA
Independent Study, P.O. Box 2967, University, AL 35486

UNIVERSITY OF ALASKA
Correspondence Study, 101-D Eielson, Fairbanks, AK 99703

UNIVERSITY OF ARIZONA
University Extension/Extended Study, 1717 East Speedway, Babcock Building 3201, Tucson, AZ 85721

UNIVERSITY OF ARKANSAS
Department of Independent Study, Division of Continuing Education, 346 West Avenue, Fayetteville, AR 72701

UNIVERSITY OF CALIFORNIA
Independent Study Department, 2223 Fulton Street, Berkeley, CA 94720

UNIVERSITY OF COLORADO
Center for Lifelong Learning, Division of Continuing Education, 970 Aurora Avenue, Room 206, Boulder, CO 80302

UNIVERSITY OF FLORIDA
Department of Correspondence Study, 2012 West University Avenue, Gainesville, FL 32603

UNIVERSITY OF GEORGIA
Georgia Center for Continuing Education, Athens, GA 30602

UNIVERSITY OF IDAHO
Correspondence Study Office, Moscow, ID 83843

UNIVERSITY OF ILLINOIS
Guided Individual Study, 104 Illini Hall, 725 South Wright Street, Champaign, IL 61820

UNIVERSITY OF IOWA
Center for Credit Programs, W400 East Hall, Iowa City, IA 52242
Also offers graduate-level courses in education.

UNIVERSITY OF KANSAS
Division of Continuing Education, Lawrence, KS 66045

UNIVERSITY OF KENTUCKY
Independent Study Program, Room 1, Frazee Hall 00031, Lexington, KY 40506

UNIVERSITY OF MICHIGAN
Extension Service, Department of Independent Study, 412 Maynard Street, Ann Arbor, MI
48109
Also offers graduate-level courses in several fields.

UNIVERSITY OF MINNESOTA
Department of Independent Study, 69 Westbrook Hall, 77 Pleasant Street, SE, Minneapolis,
MN 55455

UNIVERSITY OF MISSISSIPPI
Department of Independent Study, University, MS 38677

UNIVERSITY OF MISSOURI
Center for Independent Study Through Correspondence, 514 South Fifth Street, Columbia, MO
65211

UNIVERSITY OF NEBRASKA
Division of Continuing Studies, 511 Nebraska Hall, Lincoln, NE 68588

UNIVERSITY OF NEVADA
Extended Programs and Continuing Education, Reno, NV 89557

UNIVERSITY OF NEW MEXICO
Division of Continuing Education, 805 Yale Boulevard., Albuquerque, NM 87131

UNIVERSITY OF NORTH CAROLINA
Independent Study by Extension, 121 Abernethy 002A, Chapel Hill, NC 27514

UNIVERSITY OF NORTH DAKOTA
Correspondence Study, Box 8277, University Station, Grand Forks, ND 58202

UNIVERSITY OF NORTHERN COLORADO
Continuing Education, Greeley, CO 80639

UNIVERSITY OF NORTHERN IOWA
Extension and Continuing Education, 144 Gilchrist, Cedar Falls, IA 50613

UNIVERSITY OF OKLAHOMA
Independent Study Department, 1700 Asp, Norman, OK 73037

UNIVERSITY OF SOUTH CAROLINA
Correspondence Study, Center for Credit Programs, Columbia, SC 29208

UNIVERSITY OF SOUTH DAKOTA
Statewide Educational Services, Vermillion, SD 57069

UNIVERSITY OF SOUTHERN MISSISSIPPI
Department of Independent Study, Southern Station, Box 5056, Hattiesburg, MS 39401

UNIVERSITY OF TENNESSEE
Center for Extended Learning, 447 Communications and Extensions Building, Knoxville, TN
37916

UNIVERSITY OF TEXAS
Extension and Correspondence Studies, Education Annex F-38, Austin, TX 78712

UNIVERSITY OF UTAH
Division of Continuing Education, Correspondence Study, 1152 Annex, Salt Lake City, UT 84112

UNIVERSITY OF WASHINGTON
Independent Study, Lewis Hall, Room 212, Mail Stop DW-30, Seattle, WA 98195

UNIVERSITY OF WISCONSIN
Independent Study, 209 Extension Building, 432 North Lake Street, Madison, WI 53706
In addition to academic courses, the university offers a large number of nonacademic vocational and technical courses.

UNIVERSITY OF WYOMING
Correspondence Study, Box 3294 University Station, Laramie, WY 82071

UTAH STATE UNIVERSITY
Independent Study Division, Logan, UT 84321

WASHINGTON STATE UNIVERSITY
Continuing University Studies, 208 Van Doren Hall, Pullman, WA 99164

WESTERN MICHIGAN UNIVERSITY
Department of Continuing Education, Kalamazoo, MI 49008

WESTERN WASHINGTON UNIVERSITY
Independent Study Coordinator, Old Main 400, Bellingham, WA 98225

BIBLIOGRAPHY

BUSINESSES

Kahm, H.S., *101 Businesses You Can Start and Run With Less Than $1,000* (Parker Publishing Company, Inc.).

Levinson, Jay Conrad, *555 Ways to Earn Extra Money* (Holt, Rinehart and Winston).

Lowry, Albert J., *How to Become Financially Successful by Owning Your Own Business* (Simon and Schuster).

Revel, Chase, *168 More Businesses Anyone Can Start and Make a Lot of Money* (Bantam Books).

Woy, Patricia A., *Small Businesses That Grow and Grow and Grow* (Betterway Publications, Inc.).

CAREERS

Azrin, Nathan H., and Besalel, Victoria A., *The Job Club* (Ten Speed Press).

Azrin, Nathan H., *Finding a Job* (Ten Speed Press).

Barron's Profiles of American Colleges (Barron's Educational Series).

Bear, John, Ph.D., *How to Earn an American University Degree Without Ever Going to America* (Mendocino Book Company).

Bear, John, Ph.D., *How to Get the Degree You Want* (Ten Speed Press).

Bolles, Richard N., *The Quick Job-Hunting Map: A Fast Way to Help* (Ten Speed Press).

Bolles, Richard N., *What Color Is Your Parachute?* (Ten Speed Press).

Cass, James, and Birnbaum, Max, *Comparative Guide to American Colleges* (Harper and Row).

Cluster, Dick, and Rutter, Nancy, *Shrinking Dollars Vanishing Jobs: Why the Economy Isn't Working for You* (Beacon Press).

Crystal, John C, and Bolles, Richard N., *Where Do I Go From Here With My Life?* (Ten Speed Press).

Guide to the Evaluation of Educational Experiences in the Armed Forces (American Council on Education).

Hopke, William E. (editor), *Encyclopedia of Careers and Vocational Guidance*, Fifth Edition (Garrett Park Press).

Hunter, Joan, *Guide to Independent Study Through Correspondence Instruction* (Peterson's Guides).

International Handbook of Universities (International Association of Universities).

Kingstone, Brett, *The Student Entrepreneur's Guide* (Ten Speed Press).

Komar, John J., *The Great Escape From Your Dead-End Job* (Follett Publishing Co.).

Lathrop, Richard, *The Job Market* (The National Center for Job-Market Studies).

Lathrop, Richard, *Who's Hiring Who?* (Ten Speed Press).

Noer, David, *How to Beat the Employment Game* (Ten Speed Press).

Terkel, Studs, *Working* (Avon Paperback).

U.S. Department of Labor, Bureau of Labor Statistics, *Exploring Careers* (Superintendent of Documents).

ECONOMICS

Angly, Edward, *Oh, Yeah?* (Viking Press).

Batra, Dr. Ravi, *The Great Depression of 1990* (Dell).

Batra, Dr. Ravi, *Surviving The Great Depression of 1990* (Simon and Schuster).

Blakewell, Paul, *Thirteen Curious Errors About Money* (Caxton Printers).

Browne, Harry, *How to Profit From the Coming Devaluation* (Avon).

Browne, Harry, *Inflation Proofing Your Investments* (William Morrow).

Browne, Harry, *New Profits From the Monetary Crisis* (William Morrow).

Browne, Harry, *You Can Profit From a Monetary Crisis* (MacMillian).

Cardiff and English, *The Coming Real Estate Crash* (Arlington House).

Casey, Douglas R., *The International Man* (Pocket Books).

Casey, Douglas R., *Crisis Investing: Opportunities and Profits in the Coming Great Depression* (Pocket Books).

Casey, Douglas R., *Strategic Investing* (Pocket Books).

Colt, C.C., and Keith, N., *28 Days*, (Greenberg Publishers).

Friedman, Milton, *Capitalism & Freedom* (The University of Chicago Press).

Hazlitt, Henry, *Economics in One Lesson* (Manor Books).

Hazlitt, Henry, *The Failure of the New Economics* (Arlington House).

Hazlitt, Henry, *The Inflation Crisis* And *How to Resolve It* (Arlington House).

Leon, Sy, *None of the Above* (Fabian Press).

Naisbitt, John, *Megatrends* (Warner Books).

North, Dr. Gary, *How You Can Profit From the Coming Price Controls* (American Bureau of Economic Research).

Patterson, Robert T., *The Great Boom and Panic* (Henry Regnery Company).

Peters, Dr. Harvey, *America's Coming Bankruptcy* (Arlington House).

Pugsley, John, *Common Sense Economics* (Common Sense Press).

Pugsley, John, *The Alpha Strategy* (Common Sense Press).

Rand, Ayn, *Capitalism: The Unknown Ideal* (Signet).

Ringer, Robert J., *How You Can Find Happiness During the Collapse of Western Civilization* (QED/Harper & Row).

Ringer, Robert J., *Restoring the American Dream* (Fawcett Books).

Rothbard, Murray N.,*What Has Government Done to Our Money* (Rampart College).

Rothbard, Murray N., *America's Great Depression* (Nash Publishing).

Rothbard, Murray N., *For a New Liberty* (MacMillan).

Rothbard, Murray N., *The Coming Credit Collapse* (Sheed, Andrews & McMeel).

Rothbard, Murray N., *The Panic of 1819* (Columbia University Press).

Ruff, Howard, *How to Prosper During the Coming Bad Years* (Times Books).

Schiff, Irwin, *The Biggest Con* (Freedom Books).

Sennholz, Hans, *Age of Inflation* (Western Islands).

Smith, Jerome, *The Coming Currency Collapse* (Books in Focus).

Von Mises, Ludwig, *Human Action* (Henry Regnery).

INDEX

ASSOCIATION INDEX

NOTES

ABOUT THE AUTHOR

Roger A. Kessinger is a business consultant specializing in employee benefit plans. He can be contacted by writing to:

P.O. Box 8933
Boise, ID 83707